# Tanizaki in Western Languages

# Tanizaki in Western Languages

## A Bibliography of Translations and Studies

Adriana Boscaro

With a List of Films Based on Tanizaki's Works
Compiled by Maria Roberta Novielli

CENTER FOR JAPANESE STUDIES
THE UNIVERSITY OF MICHIGAN
ANN ARBOR, 2000

Published by the Center for Japanese Studies, The University of Michigan,
202 S. Thayer St., Ann Arbor, MI 48104-1608

The illustration that appears on the title page and is stamped on the cover is the Bussokuseiki (The Buddha's Footprints), which Munakata Shikō designed for the first edition of *Fūten rōjin nikki* (1962); it was also the logo of the International Symposium on Tanizaki held in Venice in 1995. Heartfelt thanks to the Munakata Shikō Organization for permission to use it.

Book design and typesetting by Franco A. Gatti.

**Library of Congress Cataloging-in-Publication Data**

Boscaro, Adriana

Tanizaki in western languages : a bibliography of translations and studies / Adriana Boscaro, with a list of films based on Tanizaki's works compiled by Maria Roberta Novielli.

p. cm.

Includes bibliographical references.

ISBN 0–939512–99–8 (cloth : alk. paper)

1. Tanizaki, Jun'ichirō, 1886–1965—Bibliography. 2. Tanizaki, Jun'ichirō, 1886–1965—Translations into foreign languages—Bibliography. 3. Tanizaki, Jun'ichirō, 1886–1965—Film and video adaptations. I. Novielli, Maria Roberta, 1964– List of films based on Tanizaki's works. II. Title.

Z8858.73 .B67 2000 [PL839.A7]
016.8956'344—dc21

99–049891

The paper used in this publication meets the requirements of the ANSI/NISO Standard Z39.44-1992 (Permanence of Paper for Publications and Documents in Libraries and Archives).

Printed in the United States of America

# Table of Contents



A List of Films Based on Tanizaki's Works
compiled by Maria Roberta Novielli

This work is gratefully dedicated to the memory of an old friend of Tanizaki, Shimanaka Hōji (1923–97) of Chūō Kōronsha, without whose generous help the International Symposium on Tanizaki Jun'ichirō, held in Venice on 5–8 April 1995, would not have been possible.

# Foreword

The purpose of this volume is to provide bibliographical access to those works of Tanizaki that have been translated into European languages — principally French, Italian, English, and German, but also Spanish, Czech, Finnish, Dutch, Hungarian, Polish, and others — and to facilitate research by listing relevant studies in the major European languages. This is the first such work in the West devoted to a Japanese writer, and thus it is especially fitting that it celebrates a "figure of world stature," as Donald Keene described Tanizaki some years ago.

Strangely enough, and obviously quite by accident, the year of Tanizaki's death (1965; he was born in 1886) was a significant year in the life of the Japanese Studies Institute of the University of Venice. The Institute was founded that same year and has since become one of the most important centers devoted to the study of Japan in Italy, and the one at which Tanizaki is most studied. Indeed, since 1980 some twenty translations have been produced by scholars of the Japanese Studies Institute in Venice. It was, therefore, the appropriate place to hold the First International Symposium on Tanizaki, 5-8 April 1995, a joint celebration of the thirtieth anniversary of the founding of the Institute and a commemoration of the thirtieth anniversary of the writer's death.

The Symposium brought together for the first time scholars in the field of Tanizaki studies from Europe, North America, and Japan. It was during the preparations for the meeting that I suddenly realized we lacked a bibliography of studies and translations of this important twentieth-century writer. In an attempt to fill this gap, I compiled as complete a bibliography as I could in the time available, appended a section on film adaptations, and presented the resulting booklet to participants of the Symposium as a work-in-progress. The size and range of even this preliminary listing were impressive and this encouraged me to go further. After three years spent pestering people around the world for references and materials, I can now say that the results are little short of astonishing. Although my knowledge is not as complete as it should be and though I have had to neglect some languages, Russian and Turkish for example, I can state that seventy-six works by Tanizaki have thus far been translated into Western languages. This gives a total of 263 translations in seventeen languages. The list of writings on Tanizaki includes an additional 223 items.

This bibliography confirms the universality of Tanizaki's appeal and his transcendence of time and place. The most evident sources of his popularity are his depiction of the exotic/erotic Japan that so many foreigners love to read about, his teasing of his readers, and his superb mastery of the art of storytelling. The bibliography also provokes questions. What does it mean, for example, that the early short story "Shisei" has been translated no less than twenty-six times? Why are there three different French translations, two Italian, five English, five German, two Hungarian, as well as two versions on film?

Any attempt to answer such questions would involve tracing not only the history of the study and translation of Tanizaki's works, but also their marketing and profitability for publishing houses. Who can tell why publishers felt the need for so many new translations of "Shisei"? Was it merely because it was the very first of his stories to be translated, as early as 1917, and therefore "Shisei" meant Tanizaki? Might it not also be that because "Shisei" was such a devastating story, providing Western readers with exactly the erotic-eerie atmosphere they looked to Japan for, it appealed to publishers anxious to sell more copies? This is a cynical suggestion, I admit, but experience reveals that publishers are only too well aware of the bottom line. A 1988 Italian paperback reprint of *Kagi* came wrapped in a dust jacket showing a big-breasted, rapacious-looking woman wearing a lewd expression, and an entirely invented subtitle: "Vertigine e dannazione dell'eros" (The vertiginous curse of eros). Needless to say, this attitude is not confined to Tanizaki's works; it is lamentably widespread. When Peter Greenaway's film *The Pillow Book* (1996) was released, many authoritative Italian critics affirmed that Sei Shōnagon's *Makura no sōshi* was the most important classic erotic novel of Japan, obviously confusing *The Pillow Book* with a "pillow-book," and thus revealing that they had not even opened it. But every cloud has a silver lining — Greenaway's film led to a reprint of the Italian translation of *The Pillow Book,* which had long been out of print. Just guess the subject of the dust jacket!

We are also fortunate to have publications that enlighten us, and I would like to mention two of them. In 1988, a volume of Tanizaki's work that included fifteen translations and a critical study was included in a series devoted to world classics put out by the Italian publisher Bompiani (Jun'ichirō Tanizaki, *Opere*, ed. Adriana Boscaro [Milano: Bompiani, 1988]). But the most notable achievement so far is the French edition of Tanizaki, published 1997-98, which comprises two volumes, a total of 3579 pages, in the prestigious Gallimard series *Bibliothèque de la Pléiade*. The selection contains forty-one texts, all duly introduced and annotated by a team of eminent French specialists, headed by Jacqueline Pigeot (Tanizaki, *Œuvres* 1, ed. Jacqueline Pigeot et al. [Paris: Gallimard, 1997]; Tanizaki, *Œuvres* 2, ed. Jacqueline Pigeot et al. [Paris: Gallimard, 1998]).

Here follows a short guide to this book.

The bibliography is divided into several sections. Section 1 lists the seventy-six works that can be read in translation. (The * marks translations that are not from the original.) Translations are grouped chronologically under the original Japanese titles, which are listed alphabetically. Reprints have not been included unless they are new translations, have a different title, or appear in a different book. To facilitate reading, the following abbreviations have been used to indicate the languages of the translations:

(BG) Bulgarian
(CZ) Czech
(D) German
(DK) Danish
(E) Spanish
(ENG) English
(ESP) Esperanto
(F) French
(H) Hungarian
(I) Italian
(NL) Dutch
(P) Portuguese
(PL) Polish
(S) Swedish
(SC) Serbo-Croatian
(SF) Finnish
(SL) Slovenian

Section 2 arranges these translations by language, demonstrating something of the popularity of the author in different languages, and revealing that France leads the way with a total of fifty-four different works translated.

In Section 3 the translations are arranged in chronological order by year of publication. This provides a glimpse of the ups and downs of translation activity over the years, and shows that the golden decades have been the 1960s, the 1980s, and the 1990s.

Section 4 lists the contents of collections, allowing the reader to trace a work even when its existence is "hidden" under a general title.

Section 5 is an index of translated titles, enabling easy reference when only the translated title is known.

Section 6 contains information about 223 writings on Tanizaki. Assembling this information turned out to be a rather difficult task, and I am afraid the list is limited mostly to English, French, and Italian entries. I call them "writings," and not essays, because I have also included very short pieces, chapters of books dealing with more general problems, introductions to translations, and some reviews. It is my opinion that short notes are sometimes as enlightening as long essays.

Whenever possible, the spelling of Tanizaki's name is given as it appears in the original text, so, for example, Jun'ichirō appears also as Junichiro, Junichirô, and Džuničiró.

I apologize for any omissions, and for neglecting other languages. I would be grateful to anyone who informs me of omissions or errors, and I would especially welcome any additional information about works in Western languages on, by, or related to Tanizaki.

There are no references to bibliographies of criticism and scholarship in Japanese, because I felt that any choice I made would be unfair to those omitted, and also because the focus of this bibliography is works in Western languages, not Japanese.

Section 7 is an index of translators, regardless of whether they worked from the original or not.

*A List of Films Based on Tanizaki's Works* follows, prepared by Maria Roberta Novielli, an expert on Japanese cinema. To the best of my knowledge, it is the first such comprehensive list. The films are arranged by year of release, and entries provide as much information as it has been possible to ascertain, including original story, director, screenplay writer, cinematographer, duration, and so on. Cross-references will help readers trace the titles of the original Tanizaki stories.

I am indebted to Professor Ōshima Maki of Tokyo Joshi Daigaku for helping with the correct spelling of some names and for other information.

Not being a professional bibliographer, I am sure that this work has deficiencies of a technical sort. My principal aim, however, is to demonstrate how widely Tanizaki is known around the world, and to that end a great many people helped to check titles and information. I wish to thank them all. Among those to whom I am especially indebted are Frank J. Shulman, Jürgen Stalph, Luisa Bienati, Anthony H. Chambers, Amalia Sato, András Hernády, Olof Lidin, Corrie Siahaya-Van Nierop, Rein Raud, Mikołaj Melanowicz, Judit Vihar, Maria Rodríguez del Alisal, Tzvetana Kristeva, Paola Mildonian, Vlasta Winkelhöferová, Laura Moretti, and last but not least Franco A. Gatti, my computer "magician."

Heartfelt thanks also to Gaye Rowley, who was there from the very beginning.

A. B.

October 1999

# はじめに

本書の目的は、ヨーロッパ言語に訳された谷崎潤一郎の作品の文献的資料を提供することにある。フランス語、イタリア語、英語、ドイツ語がそのおもな言語であるが、スペイン語、チェコ語、フィンランド語、オランダ語、ハンガリー語、ポーランド語なども含まれている。また、ヨーロッパの主要言語における谷崎研究の主たるものをリストにおさめ、研究者の便をはかることもめざした。この種の仕事が日本人の作家を対象としてなされるのは、西洋ではこれが最初のことであり、かつてドナルド・キーンが「世界的レベルの個性」と評した作家をたたえるにあたって、まことにふさわしい試みと思われる。

谷崎潤一郎の没年(1965年。生年は1886年)は、まったく偶然のことながら、ヴェネツィア大学日本研究科にとっても意義深い年であった。日本研究科はまさにその年に誕生し、その後、イタリアにおける日本研究のもっとも重要な機関のひとつに発展したのである。とりわけ谷崎研究はイタリアでもっとも活発で、1980年以来、ヴェネツィア大学の研究者による谷崎作品の翻訳はおよそ20に及ぶ。したがってヴェネツィアは、第一回谷崎国際シンポジウム(1995年4月5 - 8日)開催の場として最適の場であったといえよう。この機会に谷崎没後30年を記念するとともに、あわせてヴェネツィア大学日本研究科の創立30年を祝うことができたのである。

このシンポジウムにおいて、ヨーロッパ、北アメリカ、日本の谷崎研究者ははじめて一同に会する機会を得た。20世紀の誇る作家である谷崎に、翻訳、研究論文の文献目録が存在しないことに私が気づいたのは、この会議の準備を進めていたときであった。その欠除を補おうと、この機会に可能なかぎりの作品を網羅して文献目録を作成し、映画化された谷崎作品のリストも付して"work-in-progress"として会議の参加者に配付した。まがりなりにも短時間でこのような目録を仕上げることができたのに力を得て、私は情報収集を続けることにし、3年ものあいだ、世界中の友人、知人たちをわずらわして情報提供をお願いした。その結果、信じられないほどの収穫を得ることができた。残念ながらロシア語、トルコ語など、いくつかの言語を除外しなければならなかったが、76もの谷崎の作品がヨーロッパの言語に翻訳されていること、翻訳の総数は263点、17言語にのぼることがわかった。さらに本書には223もの谷崎研究をあげてある。

この文献目録からは、谷崎の名声が世界的なものであり、時間と空間を越えたものであることがわかる。谷崎のこの人気の秘訣には、疑いなく、外国人が読みたいと願うエキゾティックで官能的な日本を描いたこともあろうし、読者をもてあそぶ手腕や、あの卓越した、語りの巧みさなどもあるだろう。しかし、疑問も浮かんでくる。若い頃の作品である「刺青」が26回も翻訳されているのはなぜだろうか。しかも、フランス語訳が3篇もあり、イタリア語訳が2篇、英語、ドイツ語訳がそれぞれ5篇もあるのは、どうしたわけなのだろうか。さらに、この作品は二度も映画化されている。

この問いに答えようとすれば、谷崎文学の翻訳、研究の歴史ばかりか、出版社の営業戦略の歴史をたどることにもなろう。「刺青」のかくも多くの翻訳を世にだす必要があった理由を、誰が答えてくれるだろうか。これが谷崎の最初の短編であって、1917年にはすでに翻訳がなされており、したがって、谷崎といえば「刺青」を意味したのだろうか。あるいは、おそらく「刺青」という極端な作品が、西洋の読者が日本に対して期待する、あの官能的でどこか奇妙な雰囲気を、読む者に与えることができ、そのために利益を求める出版社に好まれたのだろうか。こういうと皮肉に聞こえるかもしれないが、出版社が宝の埋蔵地をよく知っていることは、経験が教えてくれるところである。例をあげるならば、「鍵」のイタリア語版がペーパーバックで再版されたとき、そのような必要性などまるでないのに、表紙には胸をあらわにし、みだらな表情をうかべた若い女性の姿が使われ、「目眩と苦悶のエロス」なる、でっちあげの副題がついていた。

むろん、このような扱いは谷崎にかぎったことではなく、悲しいかな、よく見られるものである。1996年に映画「ピーター・グリーナウェイの枕草子」がでたとき、イタリアでは多くの権威ある批評家たちが清少納言の「枕草子」を日本古典文学における重要な官能小説だとしていた。むろん、「枕本」と混同してのことなのだが、彼らが「枕草子」の本を開いてもみなかったことがこれによってわかる。ただ、不幸も何かの役には立つもので、この映画のおかげで、しばらく前から品切れになっていた「枕草子」のイタリア語訳が再版されることとなった。どんな表紙が選ばれたかについては、みなさんの想像におまかせしよう。

他方で意義ある出版もおこなわれている。ここではとくに二つの出版物にふれたい。ひとつは、1988年にイタリアのボンピアーニ古典叢書の一環としてだされた、15の翻訳と谷崎論ひとつをおさめた作品集である。もうひとつは、ヨーロッパにおける谷崎文学の、今日までのもっとも重要な出版である、フランス、ガリマール社のプレイヤード叢書の作品集である。1997年から98年にかけて出版された2巻からなるこの作品集は、42もの作品をおさめ、総ページ数は3579ページにおよぶ。ジャクリーン・ピジョーを監修者とし、作品にはすべて、谷崎研究の専門家たちによる解説、註がつけられている。

さて、以下にこの文献目録の構成について簡潔に説明しておく。目録は七部にわかれる。

第一部では、翻訳のある76の作品を列挙した。まずアルファベット順で原作の作品名(日本語)を記し、作品ごとに刊行年にしたがって翻訳作品を列挙した。再版は、新訳である場合、異なる題名がつけられた場合、他の本に所収された場合をのぞき、リストに入れなかった。参照の便宜をはかるために、以下のような略語をつかって、翻訳言語を示した。

(BG) ブルガリア語
(CZ) チェコ語
(D) ドイツ語
(DK) デンマーク語
(E) スペイン語
(ENG) 英語
(ESP) エスペラント語
(F) フランス語
(H) ハンガリー語
(I) イタリア語
(NL) オランダ語
(P) ポルトガル語
(PL) ポーランド語
(S) スウェーデン語
(SC) セルボ・クロアチア語
(SF) フィンランド語
(SL) スロヴェニア語

第二部では、これらの翻訳作品を言語別に並べた。これによって谷崎作品の人気の程度を国ごとにみることができる。翻訳作品数がもっとも多いのは、54作もの翻訳のあるフランスである。

第三部では翻訳作品を刊行年順に並べた。これにより、どのぐらいの翻訳がなされていたか、年代ごとに追うことができる。ちなみに、谷崎の翻訳がもっとも活発であったのは、1960年代、80年代、90年代であった。

第四部では各翻訳作品集におさめられた作品名を記し、所収の作品をさがすための便宜をはかった。

第五部は翻訳の題名による索引である。訳題から原題をさがせるようになっている。

第六部には谷崎について書かれたものを集めた。これは223点にものぼるが、このような資料についての情報を集めることは決して楽ではなく、残念ながら英語、フランス語、イタリア語にかぎらざるを得なかった。これらの文章を論文と呼ばずに著述(writings)としたのは、短い記事や、より広範な文学書の谷崎に関する章、翻訳に付された解説などをも含むためである。これにはいくつかの書評も入れたが、私は短い記述が長い論文以上に啓発してくれることもあると考えている。

第七部は、訳者名の索引である。原書からの直接の翻訳ではない場合も含んでいる。

谷崎の名前の表記にあたっては、可能なかぎり、翻訳にあらわれるものにしたがい、あえて統一することはしなかった。

気づかずにこの目録に入れ損じた作品もあろうかと思う。心からお詫びしたい。また、すべてのヨーロッパ言語をフォローできなかったことについてもお詫びする。見落とし、誤りなどはご指摘いただければ幸いである。またその他にも、欧文における谷崎に関する著作等をご存じの方は、ぜひお知らせいただきたいと思う。

日本語の文献をいっさい含まなかったのは、それがあまりに多大であって、そこから何を選択するにしても正当な選択にはなりえないこともあるが、とりわけこの文献目録が、日本語ではなく欧文に焦点をあてたものであることによる。

「谷崎作品を原作とする映画リスト」は日本映画研究を専門とするマリア・ロベルタ・ノヴィエッリによる。私が知るかぎり、これまでに知られているこの種のリストのもっとも整ったものである。映画作品を発表年順に並べ、それぞれについて原作名、監督、脚本、撮影、時間その他、収集できた情報を可能なかぎり記してある。また、原作から映画作品をさがせるように、その他のリストを付して便宜をはかった。

このリストの制作にあたり、いろいろな情報を送ってくださり、日本人名の正しい表記についてご教示くださった東京女子大学の大島眞木教授に、心から感謝したい。

私は専門の書誌家ではない。本書には正確さを欠く箇所も多々あることとは思うが、私が本書でめざしたのは、谷崎作品が世界に広く普及していることを示すことであったので、ご了承いただきたく思う。本書の編集にあたっては、多くの方々のお力を拝借した。書名、情報を寄せてくださったみなさんに心から感謝する。とくに、Frank J. Shulman, Jürgen Stalph, Luisa Bienati, Anthony H. Chambers, Amalia Sato, András Hernády, Olof Lidin, Corrie Siahaya-Van Nierop, Rein Raud, Mikołaj Melanowicz, Judit Vihar, Maria Rodríguez del Alisal, Tzvetana Kristeva, Paola Mildonian, Vlasta Winkelhöferová, Laura Moretti そして最後になったが、コンピューターの魔術師、Franco A. Gattiに、この場をかりてお礼申し上げる。

また、この仕事の始めから常に協力を惜しまなかったGaye Rowleyに心から感謝したい。

1999 年 10 月　　A. B.

（中山悦子訳）

# 1

# Translations

"A to B no hanashi" AとBの話 (1921)

1997 (F) "Histoire de A et B," trans. Patrick De Vos. In Tanizaki, *Œuvres* 1, 507-50. Paris: Gallimard.

*Aisureba koso* 愛すればこそ (1921)

1925 (F) *Puisque je l'aime,* trans. S. Asada, H. Yokohama, and Charles Jacob. Paris: Emile-Paul Frères.

1929 (I) **Io l'amo!*, trans. Lorenzo Gigli. Milano: Alpes.

1930 (E) *Amor*, trans. Antonio Ferratges. In *Teatro japones*, ed. Cristobal de Castro. Madrid: J. Pueyo.

1940 (I) **Poiché io l'amo…*, trans. Lorenzo Gigli. *Il Dramma* 16.344 (15 December), 5-29.

"Akuma" 悪魔 (1912)

1986 (I) "Il demone" (Prima parte), trans. Lydia Origlia. In Jun'ichirō Tanizaki, *Il dramma stregato*, 9-30. Milano: SE.

*Amachua kurabu* アマチュア倶楽部 (1921), scenario

1995 (I) *Amateur Club*, trans. Cinzia Mottola. In Tanizaki Jun'ichirō, *Divagazioni sull'otium e altri scritti*, ed. Adriana Boscaro, 113-57. Venezia: Cafoscarina.

"Aoi hana" 青い花 (1922)

1963 (ENG) "Aguri," trans. Howard Hibbett. In Junichiro Tanizaki, *Seven Japanese Tales*, 186-204. New York: Alfred A. Knopf. First appeared as "Western Mannequin on the Ginza," in *Cosmopolitan* 155.2 (August 1963), 85-89.

1966 (SF) *"Aguri," trans. Kai Kaila. In Tanizaki Junichirō, *Unien silta*, 163-79. Helsinki: Tammi.

1994 (E) *"La flor azul," trans. Amalia Sato. *Tokonoma* 1 (Summer), 48-57.

1994 (D) "Aguri," trans. Bernhard Straub. In *Blut in der Morgenröte: Japanische Kriminalstories 3,* ed. Janwillem van de Wetering, 143-58. Reinbek bei Hamburg: Rowohlt (rororo thriller 3075).

"Aozukashi no hanashi" 青塚氏の話 (1926)

1991 (F) "Monsieur Aozuka," trans. Marc Mécréant. In Junichirô Tanizaki, *L'affaire du "Yanagiyu" et autres récits étranges*, 281-325. Paris: Gallimard.

"Aru shōnen no osore" ある少年の怯れ (1919)

1997 (F) "Affres d'un jeune garçon," trans. Marc Mécréant. In Tanizaki, *Œuvres* 1, 459-505. Paris: Gallimard.

*Ashikari* 蘆刈 (1932)

1936 (ENG) *Ashikari*, trans. Roy Humpherson and Hajime Okita. In Junichiro Tanizaki, *Ashikari and The Story of Shunkin*, 1-67. Tokyo: Hokuseido. In 1935 an abridged version circulated as a mimeo copy in Shanghai.

1960 (F) *Ashikari: un couple dans les roseaux*, trans. Kikou Yamata. In Junichiro Tanizaki, *Deux amours cruelles*, 91-139. Paris: Stock (abridged version).

1963 (I) *I canneti*, trans. Giuseppe Ricca and Atsuko Ricca Suga. In Junichiro Tanizaki, *Due amori crudeli*, 97-157. Milano: Bompiani. Reprinted in Tanizaki, *Opere,* 553-98. Milano: Bompiani, 1988. Reprinted in Junichiro Tanizaki, *Il ponte dei sogni e altri racconti*, 39-88. Milano: Bompiani, 1995.

1968 (E) **Ashikari*, trans. Jesús López Pacheco. In Junichiro Tanizaki, *Cuentos crueles*, 65-99. Barcelona: Seix Barral.

1971 (PL) *Ashikari, czyli źle mi bez ciebie*, trans. Mikołaj Melanowicz. In Tanizaki Jun'ichirō, *Dwie opowieści o miłości okrutnej*, 7-75. Warszawa: Państwowy Instytut Wydawniczy.

1983 (CZ) *Požaté rákosí*, trans. Vlasta Winkelhöferová. In Džuničiró Tanizaki, *Most snů*, 17-55. Praha: Vyšehrad.

1994 (ENG) *The Reed Cutter,* trans. Anthony H. Chambers. In *Two Novellas by Junichirō Tanizaki—The Reed Cutter and Captain Shigemoto's Mother,* 1-53. New York: Alfred A. Knopf.

1997 (F) *Le coupeur de roseaux*, trans. Daniel Struve. In Tanizaki, *Œuvres* 1, 1347-92. Paris: Gallimard.

"Ave Maria" アヱ・マリア (1923)

1995 (I) "Ave Maria," trans. Luisa Bienati. In Tanizaki Jun'ichirō, *I piedi di Fumiko—Ave Maria*, ed. Luisa Bienati, 47-144. Venezia: Marsilio.

*Bushūkō hiwa* 武州公秘話 (1932)

1970 (I) *Vita segreta del signore di Bushu*, trans. Atsuko Ricca Suga. In Junichiro Tanizaki, *Vita segreta del signore di Bushu*, 5-181. Milano: Bompiani. Reprinted in Tanizaki, *Opere,* 401-551. Milano: Bompiani, 1988.

1982 (ENG) *The Secret History of the Lord of Musashi*, trans. Anthony H. Chambers. In *Two Novellas by Junichirō Tanizaki—The Secret History of the Lord of Musashi and Arrowroot*, 1-142. New York: Alfred A. Knopf.

1984 (E) **La historia secreta del señor de Musashi*, trans. Néstor Dietrich. In Junichiro Tanizaki, *La historia secreta del señor de Musashi/Arrurruz*. Buenos Aires: Editorial Sudamericana.

1986 (NL) *Het geheim van de heer van Musashi*, trans. C. M. Steegers-Groeneveld. Amsterdam: Meulenhoff.

1987 (F) *La vie secrète du seigneur de Musashi*, trans. René de Ceccatty and Ryôji Nakamura. In Junichirô Tanizaki, *La vie secrète du seigneur de Musashi, suivi de Le lierre de Yoshino*, 9-155. Paris: Gallimard.

1989 (E) *La vida enmascarada del señor de Musashi*, trans. Fernando Rodríguez-Izquierdo. In Junichiroo Tanizaki, *La vida enmascarada del señor de Musashi / Enredadera de Yoshino*. Barcelona: Ed. Edhasa.

1994 (D) *Die geheime Geschichte des Fürsten von Musashi*, trans. Josef Bohaczek. Frankfurt: Insel Verlag.

1996 (PL) *Tajemna historia pana Musashiego*, trans. Krystyna Piórkowska. Warszawa: Państwowy Instytut Wydawniczy.

1997 (F) *Histoire secrète du sire de Musashi*, trans. Marc Mécréant. In Tanizaki, *Œuvres* 1, 1207-346. Paris: Gallimard.

*Byakko no yu* 白狐の湯 (1923)

1930 (ENG) *The White Fox*, trans. Eric S. Bell and Eiji Ukai. In *Eminent authors of contemporary Japan*, vol. 1, 1-37. Tokyo: Kaitakusha.

1997 (F) *La source au renard blanc*, trans. Jean-Jacques Tschudin. In Tanizaki, *Œuvres* 1, 573-96. Paris: Gallimard.

"Byōjoku no gensō" 病蓐の幻想 (1916)

1997 (F) "Visions d'un lit de douleur," trans. Cécile Sakai. In Tanizaki, *Œuvres* 1, 239-62. Paris: Gallimard.

"Chiisana ōkoku" 小さな王国 (1918)

1975 (D) "Ein kleines Königreich," trans. Jürgen Berndt and Eiko Saito-Berndt. In *Träume aus zehn Nächten: Moderne japanische Erzählungen*, ed. Jürgen Berndt, 159-92. Berlin: Aufbau-Verlag.

1990 (ENG) "The Little Kingdom," trans. Paul McCarthy. In Jun'ichiro Tanizaki, *A Cat, a Man, and Two Women*, 101-35. Tokyo: Kodansha International.

1994 (F) "Le petit royaume," trans. Cécile Sakai. In Junichirô Tanizaki, *Le chat, son maître et ses deux maîtresses—Nouvelles*, 117-56. Paris: Gallimard. Reprinted in Tanizaki, *Œuvres* 1, 377-405. Paris: Gallimard, 1997.

*Chijin no ai* 痴人の愛 (1924)

1967 (I) *L'amore di uno sciocco*, trans. Carlo De Dominicis. Milano: Bompiani. Reprinted in Tanizaki, *Opere*, 157-400. Milano: Bompiani, 1988.

1970 (D) *Naomi, oder Eine unersättliche Liebe*, trans. Oscar Benl. Reinbek bei Hamburg: Rowohlt (rororo 1335).

1985 (ENG) *Naomi*, trans. Anthony H. Chambers. New York: Knopf.

1986 (P) *Naomi*, trans. Sônia Coutinho. São Paulo: Editora Brasiliense.

1988 (F) *Un amour insensé*, trans. Marc Mécréant. Paris: Gallimard. Reprinted in Tanizaki, *Œuvres* 1, 597-810. Paris: Gallimard, 1997.

"Dokutan" 獨探 (1915)

1997 (F) "L'Espion du Kaiser," trans. Jean-Jacques Tschudin. In Tanizaki, *Œuvres* 1, 197-237. Paris: Gallimard.

*Eien no gūzō* 永遠の偶像 (1922)

1925 (F) *L'Eternelle Idole*, trans. Juntarô Maruyama. *La Semeuse*, nos. 6-10 (Juin-Octobre). Reprinted in Jun'ichirô Tanizaki, *Mumyô et Aizen*, 77-181 (with parallel translation). Tokyo: Hakusuisha, 1927.

"Fumiko no ashi" 富美子の足 (1919)

1986 (F) "Le pied de Fumiko," trans. Madeleine Lévy. In *Anthologie de nouvelles japonaises contemporaines*, vol. 1, 87-117. Paris: Gallimard. Reprinted in Tanizaki, *Œuvres* 1, 431-58. Paris: Gallimard, 1997.

1995 (I) "I piedi di Fumiko," trans. Luisa Campagnol. In Tanizaki Jun'ichirō, *I piedi di Fumiko—Ave Maria,* ed. Luisa Bienati, 6-45. Venezia: Marsilio.

"Futari no chigo" 二人の稚児 (1918)

1940 (F) "Les deux novices," trans. N. Matsudaira, *France-Japon* 47 (Février): 103-10.

1997 (F) "Les deux novices," trans. Jacqueline Pigeot. In Tanizaki, *Œuvres* 1, 353-75. Paris: Gallimard.

1999 (I) "I due novizi," trans. Lydia Origlia. In Jun'ichirō Tanizaki, *Nostalgia della madre*, 67-95. Milano: SE.

*Fūten rōjin nikki* 瘋癲老人日記 (1962)

1965 (I) *Diario di un vecchio pazzo*, trans. Atsuko Ricca Suga. Milano: Bompiani. Reprinted in Tanizaki, *Opere,* 989-1134. Milano: Bompiani, 1988.

1965 (ENG) *Diary of a Mad Old Man*, trans. Howard Hibbett. New York: Knopf.

1966 (D) *Tagebuch eines alten Narren*, trans. Oscar Benl. Reinbek bei Hamburg: Rowohlt.

1967 (F) *Journal d'un vieux fou*, trans. Georges [Gaston] Renondeau. Paris: Gallimard.

1968 (NL) **Dagboek van een oude dwaas*, trans. M. Coutinho and L. Coutinho. Amsterdam: De Bezige Bij.

1972 (PL) *Dziennik szalonego starca*, trans. Mikołaj Melanowicz. In Tanizaki Jun'ichirō, *Dziennik szalonego starca: Niektórzy wolą pokrzywy,* 7-154. Warszawa: Państwowy Instytut Wydawniczy.

1980 (H) **Egy hibbant vénember naplója*, trans. Göncz Arpád. Budapest: Európa.

1998 (CZ) *Deník bláznivého starce*, trans. Anthony V. Liman. Praha: Mladá fronta.

1998 (F) *Journal d'un vieux fou*, trans. Cécile Sakai. In Tanizaki, *Œuvres* 2, 1257-387. Paris: Gallimard.

"Geidan" 藝談 (1933)

1995 (I) "Chiacchierata sull'arte," trans. Bonaventura Ruperti. In Tanizaki Jun'ichirō, *Divagazioni sull'otium e altri scritti*, ed. Adriana Boscaro, 229-76. Venezia: Cafoscarina.

"Haha o kouru ki" 母を戀ふる記 (1919)

1951 (ENG) "The house where I was born," trans. S. G. Brickley. In *The writing of idiomatic English*, 118-129. Tokyo: Kenkyūsha.

1980 (ENG) "Longing for Mother," trans. Edward Fowler. *Monumenta Nipponica* 35.4 (1980): 467-78.

1983 (CZ) "O touze po matce," trans. Vlasta Winkelhöferová. In Džuničiró Tanizaki, *Most snů,* 59-77. Praha: Vyšehrad.

1997 (F) "Nostalgie de ma mère," trans. Jacqueline Pigeot. In Tanizaki, *Œuvres* 1, 407-30. Paris: Gallimard.

1999 (I) "Nostalgia della madre," trans. Lydia Origlia. In Jun'ichirō Tanizaki, *Nostalgia della madre*, 97-120. Milano: SE.

*Hakuchūkigo* 白晝鬼語 (1918)

1994 (I) *Morbose fantasie*, trans. Cinzia Mottola. Milano: SE.

"Hassan Kan no yōjutsu" ハッサン・カンの妖術 (1917)

1991 (F) "Hassan Khan le magicien," trans. Marc Mécréant. In Junichirô Tanizaki, *L'affaire du "Yanagiyu" et autres récits étranges*, 207-54. Paris: Gallimard.

"Himitsu" 秘密 (1911)

1927 (F) "Le secret," trans. Serge Elisséev. In *Le jardin des pivoines par Nagaï Kafû, suivi de cinq récits d'écrivains japonais contemporains*, 117-46. Paris: Au Sans Pareil.

1985 (I) "Il segreto," trans. Adriana Boscaro. In Jun'ichirō Tanizaki, *Pianto di sirena e altri racconti*, 45-65. Milano: Feltrinelli. First published in *Il Giappone* 32 ([1982] 1984): 51-71. Reprinted in Tanizaki, *Opere,* 81-103. Milano: Bompiani, 1988.

1993 (ENG) "The Secret," trans. Anthony Hood Chambers. In *New Leaves: Studies and Translations of Japanese Literature in Honor of Edward Seidensticker*, ed. Aileen Gatten and Anthony H. Chambers, 157-73. Michigan Monograph Series in Japanese Studies 11. Ann Arbor: Center for Japanese Studies, The University of Michigan.

1997 (F) "Le secret," trans. Marc Mécréant. In Tanizaki, *Œuvres* 1, 61-81. Paris: Gallimard.

"Hitofusa no kami" 一と房の髪 (1926)

1997 (F) "La mèche," trans. Anne Bayard-Sakai. In Tanizaki, *Œuvres* 1, 923-39. Paris: Gallimard.

"Hōkan" 幇間 (1911)

1966 (ENG) "The Professional Jester," trans. Edilberto N. Alegre. *Asian Studies* 4.1 (University of the Philippines): 59-69.

1982 (BG) "Komediantat," trans. Vera Vutova. In Tanizaki Jun'ichirō, *Portret na Shunkin*, 134-54. Sofia: Narodna Kultura.

1985 (I) "Buffone di professione," trans. Adriana Boscaro. In Jun'ichirō Tanizaki, *Pianto di sirena e altri racconti*, 30-44. Milano: Feltrinelli. Reprinted in Tanizaki, *Opere,* 63-79. Milano: Bompiani, 1988.

"Hyōfū" 飆風 (1911)

1995 (I) "Turbine," trans. Paola Montanaro. In Tanizaki Jun'ichirō, *Divagazioni sull'otium e altri scritti*, ed. Adriana Boscaro, 33-67. Venezia: Cafoscarina.

*In'ei raisan* 陰翳禮讃 (1933)

1977 (ENG) *In Praise of Shadows*, trans. Thomas J. Harper and Edward G. Seidensticker. New Haven: Leete's Island Books.

1977 (F) *Éloge de l'ombre*, trans. René Sieffert. Paris: Publications Orientalistes de France. Reprinted in Tanizaki, *Œuvres* 1, 1469-512. Paris: Gallimard.

1982 (I) *Libro d'ombra*, trans. Atsuko Ricca Suga, ed. Giovanni Mariotti. Milano: Bompiani. Reprinted in Tanizaki, *Opere,* 671-726. Milano: Bompiani, 1988.

1987 (D) *Lob des Schattens*, trans. Eduard Klopfenstein. Zürich: Manesse.

1994 (E) **Elogio de la sombra*, trans. Julia Escobar. Madrid: Ed. Siruela.

1994 (NL) *Lof der schaduw*, trans. Pim de Vroomen. Amsterdam: Meulenhoff.

1998 (CZ) *Chvála stínů*, trans. Vlasta Winkelhöferová. Košice: Knižná dielňa Timotej.

"Itansha no kanashimi" 異端者の悲しみ (1917)

1997 (F) "Morosités d'un hérétique," trans. Marc Mécréant. In Tanizaki, *Œuvres* 1, 289-352. Paris: Gallimard.

1999 (I) "La tristezza di un eretico," trans. Lydia Origlia. In Jun'ichirō Tanizaki, *Nostalgia della madre*, 11-65. Milano: SE.

"Jinmenso" 人面疽 (1918)

1991 (F) "La tumeur à face humaine," trans. Marc Mécréant. In Junichirô Tanizaki, *L'affaire du "Yanagiyu" et autres récits étranges*, 37-62. Paris: Gallimard.

*Jōtarō* 饒太郎 (1914)

1994 (I) *Jōtarō*, trans. Emanuele Ciccarella. In Jun'ichirō Tanizaki, *Il veleno di Afrodite*, 89-177. Milano: Garzanti.

*Kagi* 鍵 (1956)

1960 (ENG) *The Key*, trans. Howard Hibbett. New York: Knopf.
1961 (D) *Der Schlüssel*, trans. Sachiko Yatsushiro and Gerhard Knauss. Reinbek bei Hamburg: Rowohlt.
1961 (SF) *Avain*, trans. Tuomas Anhava. Helsinki: Tammi.
1962 (DK) **Nøglen*, trans. Tom Kristensen. København: Grafisk Forlag.
1962 (S) **Nyckeln*, trans. Ruth Edlund. Stockholm: Walhström & Widstrand.
1962 (NL) *De sleutel*, trans. M. Coutinho. Amsterdam: De Bezige Bij.
1963 (I) *La chiave*, trans. Satoko Toguchi. Milano: Bompiani. Reprinted in Tanizaki, *Opere,* 823-929. Milano: Bompiani, 1988.
1963 (F) *La confession impudique*, trans. Gaston Renondeau. Paris: Gallimard.
1969 (SC) *Ključ*, trans. Ljiljana Čalovska. Beograd: Rad.
1990 (H) **A Kulcs*, trans. Kolozsvári Papp László. Budapest: Európa.
1994 (BG) *Klyuchat*, trans. Dora Barova. Sofia: Obsidian.
1998 (F) *La Clef*, trans. Anne Bayard-Sakai. In Tanizaki, *Œuvres* 2, 1019-122. Paris: Gallimard.

"Ken'etsukan" 検閲官 (1921)

1995 (I) "Il censore," trans. Paola Montanaro. In Tanizaki Jun'ichirō, *Divagazioni sull'otium e altri scritti*, ed. Adriana Boscaro, 81-111. Venezia: Cafoscarina.

"Kin to gin" 金と銀 (1918)

1991 (F) "L'or et l'argent," trans. Marc Mécréant. In Junichirô Tanizaki, *L'affaire du "Yanagiyu" et autres récits étranges*, 63-154. Paris: Gallimard.

"Kirin" 麒麟 (1910)

1985 (I) "Kirin," trans. Adriana Boscaro. In Jun'ichirō Tanizaki, *Pianto di sirena e altri racconti*, 16-29. Milano: Feltrinelli. First published in *Il Giappone* 20 ([1980] 1982): 73-92. Reprinted in Tanizaki, *Opere,* 13-28. Milano: Bompiani, 1988.
1986 (F) "Le Ki-lin," trans. Groupe Kirin. In *Les noix La mouche Le citron et dix autres récits de l'époque Taishô*, 195-215. N.p.: Editions Picquier-Le Calligraphe.
1997 (F) "Le Kilin," trans. Jean-Jacques Tschudin and Jacqueline Pigeot. In Tanizaki, *Œuvres* 1, 13-26. Paris: Gallimard.

"Konjiki no shi" 金色の死 (1914)

1995 (I) *La morte d'oro*, trans. Luisa Bienati. Venezia: Marsilio.
1997 (F) "Une mort dorée," trans. Cécile Sakai. In Tanizaki, *Œuvres* 1, 101-29. Paris: Gallimard.

"Kozō no yume" 小僧の夢 (1917)

1994 (D) "Traum eines Ladenjungen," trans. Matthias Hoop. In *Doppelspiel der Narration: Text, Autor und Protagonist in der Erzählung "Kozō no yume" von Tanizaki Jun'ichirō*, 30-64.

Iaponia Insula, Studien zu Kultur und Gesellschaft Japans 2. Wiesbaden: Harrassowitz Verlag.

"Kyakugirai" 客ぎらひ (1948)

1982 (BG) "Samozivetzat," trans. Vera Vutova. In Tanizaki Jun'ichirō, *Portret na Shunkin*, 155-67. Sofia: Narodna Kultura.

"Kyōfu" 恐怖 (1913)

1963 (ENG) "Terror," trans. Howard Hibbett. In Junichiro Tanizaki, *Seven Japanese Tales*, 85-94. New York: Alfred A. Knopf.

1966 (SF) *"Kauhu," trans. Kai Kaila. In Tanizaki Jun'ichirō, *Unien silta*, 77-84. Helsinki: Tammi.

1968 (E) *"Terror," trans. Ángel Crespo. In Junichiro Tanizaki, *Cuentos crueles*, 101-10. Barcelona: Seix Barral.

1982 (BG) "Uzas," trans. Vera Vutova. In Tanizaki Jun'ichirō, *Portret na Shunkin*, 95-104. Sofia: Narodna Kultura.

1997 (F) "Terreur," trans. Anne Bayard-Sakai. In Tanizaki, *Œuvres* 1, 83-90. Paris: Gallimard.

"Kyōto o omou" 京都を想ふ (1962)

1997 (F) "Nostalgie de Kyôto," trans. Marc Mécréant. In *Le Vase de béryl: Études sur le Japon et la Chine en hommage à Bernard Frank*, ed. Jacqueline Pigeot and Hartmut O. Rotermund, 453-56. Arles: Philippe Picquier.

"Majutsushi" 魔術師 (1917)

1985 (I) "Il prestigiatore," trans. Adriana Boscaro. In Jun'ichirō Tanizaki, *Pianto di sirena e altri racconti*, 89-112. Milano: Feltrinelli. Reprinted in Tanizaki, *Opere,* 131-56. Milano: Bompiani, 1988.

*Mandorin o hiku otoko* マンドリンを弾く男 (1925)

1972 (ENG) *The Man with the Mandoline*, trans. Donald Keene. *New Directions* 24: 205-12.

*Manji* 卍 (1928)

1982 (I) *La croce buddista*, trans. Lydia Origlia. Milano: Guanda.

1985 (F) *Svastika*, trans. René de Ceccatty and Ryôji Nakamura. Paris: Gallimard.

1989 (NL) *Kruisende lijnen*, trans. Jacques Westerhoven. Amsterdam: Meulenhoff.

1994 (ENG) *Quicksand*, trans. Howard Hibbett. New York: Knopf.

*Mōmoku monogatari* 盲目物語 (1931)

1935-36 (F) *Récit d'un aveugle*, trans. Kiyoko Taniguchi. *Cultural Nippon* 3.4 (December 1935): 620-41; 4.1 (March 1936): 79-90; 4.2 (July 1936): 183-99; 4.3 (November 1936): 289-307.

1963 (ENG) *A Blind Man's Tale*, trans. Howard Hibbett. In Junichiro Tanizaki, *Seven Japanese Tales*, 205-98. New York: Alfred A. Knopf.

1966 (SF) **Sokean miehen kertomus*, trans. Kai Kaila. In Tanizaki Junichirō, *Unien silta*, 180-256. Helsinki: Tammi.

1968 (E) **Un cuento de ciego*, trans. Ángel Crespo. In Junichiro Tanizaki, *Cuentos crueles*, 193-272. Barcelona: Seix Barral.

1970 (I) *Racconto d'un cieco*, trans. Atsuko Ricca Suga. In Junichiro Tanizaki, *Vita segreta del signore di Bushu*, 183-286. Milano: Bompiani.

1979 (D) *Die Erzählung eines Blinden*, trans. Reinhild Böhnke. In Tanizaki Jun'ichiro, *Die Traumbrücke*, 59-135. Berlin: Volk und Welt.

1983 (CZ) *Slepcův příběh*, trans. Vlasta Winkelhöferová. In Džuničiró Tanizaki, *Most snů*, 131-201. Praha: Vyšehrad.

1997 (F) *Le récit de l'aveugle*, trans. Jacqueline Pigeot. In Tanizaki, *Œuvres* 1, 1125-206. Paris: Gallimard.

*Mumyō to Aizen* 無明と愛染 (1924)

1927 (F) *Mumyô et Aizen*, trans. Juntarô Maruyama. In Tanizaki Junichirô, *Mumyô et Aizen*, 77-175 (with parallel translation). Tokyo: Hakusuisha.

1968 (ESP) *Mumyô kaj Aizen*, trans. Teruhiko Isiguro. In Tanizaki Junichiro, *El la vivo de Syunkin*, 25-46. Osaka: Librejo Pirato.

1997 (F) *Mumyô et Aizen*, trans. Marc Mécréant. In Tanizaki, *Œuvres* 1, 811-30. Paris: Gallimard.

*Neko to Shōzō to futari no onna* 猫と庄造と二人のをんな (1936)

1970 (I) *La gatta, Shozo e le due donne*, trans. Atsuko Ricca Suga. In Junichiro Tanizaki, *Vita segreta del signore di Bushu*, 287-389. Milano: Bompiani. Reprinted in Tanizaki, *Opere*, 727-821. Milano: Bompiani, 1988.

1988 (ENG) *A Cat, Shozo and Two Women*, trans. Matsui Sakuko. University of Sydney East Asian Series. New South Wales: Wild Peony.

1990 (ENG) *A Cat, a Man, and Two Women*, trans. Paul McCarthy. In Tanizaki Jun'ichirō, *A Cat, a Man, and Two Women*, 1-99. Tokyo: Kodansha International.

1994 (F) *Le chat, son maître et ses deux maîtresses*, trans. Cécile Sakai. In Junichirô Tanizaki, *Le chat, son maître et ses deux maîtresses—Nouvelles*, 9-115. Paris: Gallimard. Reprinted in Tanizaki, *Œuvres* 1, 1513-92. Paris: Gallimard, 1997.

1996 (D) *Eine Katze, ein Mann und zwei Fraue: Novelle*, trans. Josef Bohaczek. Reinbeck: Rowohlt.

"Nihon ni okeru Kurippun jiken" 日本に於けるクリップン事件 (1927)

1995 (I) "Un 'caso Crippen' giapponese," trans. Alessandra Trombetta. In Tanizaki Jun'ichirō, *Divagazioni sull'otium e altri scritti*, ed. Adriana Boscaro, 159-73. Venezia: Cafoscarina.

"Ningyo no nageki" 人魚の嘆き (1917)

1985 (I) "Pianto di sirena," trans. Adriana Boscaro. In Jun'ichiro Tanizaki, *Pianto di sirena e altri racconti*, 66-88. Milano: Feltrinelli. First published in *Il Giappone* 24 ([1984] 1985): 65-93, with the original illustrations. Reprinted in Tanizaki, *Opere*, 105-29. Milano: Bompiani, 1988.

1997 (F) "La Complainte de la sirène," trans. Jean-Jacques Tschudin. In Tanizaki, *Œuvres* 1, 263-88. Paris: Gallimard.

"Norowareta gikyoku" 呪はれた戯曲 (1919)

1986 (I) "Il dramma stregato," trans. Lydia Origlia. In Jun'ichirō Tanizaki, *Il dramma stregato*, 123-60. Milano: SE.

1991 (F) "Un drame maudit," trans. Marc Mécréant. In Junichirô Tanizaki, *L'affaire du "Yanagiyu" et autres récits étranges*, 155-205. Paris: Gallimard.

*Okuni to Gohei* お國と五平 (1922)

1924 (ENG) *Okuni and Gohei*, trans. Isamu Suzuno. *The Tokyo Nichi Nichi* (20 September).

1931 (ENG) *Okuni and Gohei*, trans. Eric S. Bell and Eiji Ukai. In *Eminent Authors of Contemporary Japan*, 1-29. Tokyo: Kaitakusha.

1968 (ESP) *Okuni kaj Gohei*, trans. Teruhiko Isiguro. In *El la vivo de Syunkin*, 7-24. Osaka: Librejo Pirato.
1997 (F) *O-Kuni et Gohei*, trans. Jean-Jacques Tschudin. In Tanizaki, *Œuvres* 1, 551-71. Paris: Gallimard.

*Otsuya koroshi* お艶殺し (1915)
1927 (ENG) *A Springtime Case*, trans. Iwado Zenchi. Tokyo: The Japan Times.
1942 (CZ) *Milenci z Jeda*, trans. Vlasta Hilská. In *Milenci z Jeda*, 213-306. Praha: Melantrich.
1986 (I) *L'assassinio di O-Tsuya*, trans. Lydia Origlia. In Jun'ichirō Tanizaki, *Il dramma stregato*, 67-121. Milano: SE.
1997 (F) *Le meurtre d'O-Tsuya*, trans. Jean-Jacques Tschudin. In Tanizaki, *Œuvres* 1, 131-96. Paris: Gallimard.

"Radō sensei" 蘿洞先生 (1925)
1990 (ENG) "Professor Rado," trans. Paul McCarthy. In Jun'ichiro Tanizaki, *A Cat, a Man, and Two Women*, 137-64. Tokyo: Kodansha International.
1994 (F) "Le professeur Radô," trans. Jean-Jacques Tschudin. In Junichirô Tanizaki, *Le chat, son maître et ses deux maîtresses—Nouvelles*, 157-73. Paris: Gallimard. Reprinted in Tanizaki, *Œuvres* 1, 831-42. Paris: Gallimard, 1997.

"Randa no setsu" 懶惰の説 (1930)
1995 (I) "Divagazioni sull'otium," trans. Rossella Pedrini. In Tanizaki Jun'ichirō, *Divagazioni sull'otium e altri scritti*, ed. Adriana Boscaro, 175-92. Venezia: Cafoscarina.
1996 (F) "De la paresse," trans. Anne Sakai. In *Cent Ans de Pensée au Japon*, ed. Yves-Marie Allioux. Vol. 1, 169-88. Arles: Editions Philippe Picquier.

"Ren'ai oyobi shikijō" 戀愛及び色情 (1931)
1995 (I) "Amore e passione," trans. Giuliana Cavina. In Tanizaki Jun'ichirō, *Divagazioni sull'otium e altri scritti*, ed. Adriana Boscaro, 193-227. Venezia: Cafoscarina.

"Sakana no Ri Taihaku" 魚の李太白 (1918)
1921-22 (ENG) "The piscatorial Li Tai-po," trans. Glenn W. Shaw. *Eigo Seinen* 46.2-9, in eight parts.
1995 (I) "Li Bo, il pesce," trans. Adriana Boscaro. In Tanizaki Jun'ichirō, *Divagazioni sull'otium e altri scritti*, ed. Adriana Boscaro, 69-79. Venezia: Cafoscarina.

*Sasameyuki* 細雪 (1948)
1957 (ENG) *The Makioka Sisters*, trans. Edward G. Seidensticker. New York: Alfred A. Knopf. Reprinted with an introduction by Edward G. Seidensticker. New York: Alfred A. Knopf, 1993.
1961 (I) **Neve sottile*, trans. Olga Ceretti Borsini and Kizu Hasegawa. Milano: Martello. Reprinted Milano: Longanesi, 1973; Milano: Guanda, 1990.
1964 (D) *Die Schwestern Makioka*, trans. Sachiko Yatsushiro and Ulla Hengst. Reinbek bei Hamburg: Rowohlt.
1964 (F) *Quatre soeurs*, trans. Gaston Renondeau. Paris: Gallimard.
1966 (E) **Las hermanas Makioka*, trans. M. Menéndez Cuspinera. Barcelona: Seix Barral.
1967 (SL) *Sestre Makiokove*, trans. Alenka Bole-Vrabec. Ljubljana: Cankarjeva Zalozba.
1972 (SC) *Sestre Makioka*, trans. Aleksandar Petrovič. Beograd: Prosveta.
1977 (CZ) *Sestry Makiokovy*, trans. Vlasta Winkelhöferová. Praha: Svoboda.
1991 (SF) *Makiokan sisarukset*, trans. Kai Nieminen. Helsinki: Tammi.

1994 (NL) *Stille sneeuwval: de geschiedenis van de gezusters Makioka*, trans. Jacques Westerhoven. Amsterdam: Meulenhoff.

1998 (F) *Bruine de neige*, trans. Marc Mécréant, revised by Anne Bayard-Sakai. In Tanizaki, *Œuvres* 2, 1-694. Paris: Gallimard.

"Shanhai kōyūki" 上海交遊記 (1926)

1997 (ENG) "Shanghai Friends," trans. Paul D. Scott. *Chinese Studies in History* 30.4 (Summer): 71-103.

(This issue bears an additional title: "Japanese Travelogues of China in the 1920s: The Accounts of Akutagawa Ryūnosuke and Tanizaki Jun'ichirō," and was produced under the guest editorship of Joshua A. Fogel.)

*Shinzei* 信西 (1911)

1924 (ENG) *Shinzei*, trans. Glenn W. Shaw. *The Tokyo Nichi Nichi* (10-13 July).

1995 (I) *Shinzei*, trans. Adriana Boscaro. In Tanizaki Jun'ichirō, *Divagazioni sull'otium e altri scritti*, ed. Adriana Boscaro, 19-31. Venezia: Cafoscarina.

"Shisei" ("Irezumi") 刺青 (1910)

1917 (ENG) "The Young Tattooer," trans. Miyamori Asatarô. In *Representative Tales of Japan*, 1-19. Tokyo: Sanko shoin.

1923 (ENG) "Shisei," trans. Sumimasa Ijichi. *Herald of Asia* (7 April).

1924 (F) "Le tatouage," trans. Serge Elisséev. *Japon et Extrême-Orient* 2 (January 1924): 116-29. Reprinted in *Neuf Nouvelles Japonaises*, 17-30. Paris: G. van Œst, 1924. Reprinted in *Neuf Nouvelles Japonaises*, 27-45. N.p.: le calligraphe, 1984.

1925 (D) "Tätowierkunst," trans. Kenji Koike. In *Zwei Skizzen von S. Natsume* (Supplement), 1-49. Tokyo: Nankodo.

1930 (D) "Irezumi," trans. Heinz Brasch. *Yamato*: Zeitschrift der deutsch-japanischen Gesellschaft, 2.1: 8-15. Reprinted in *Japanische Geschichten* [*Geschichten und Erzählungen aus Japan*], ed. Paul Hass and Binko Matsuoka, 170-79. Leipzig: Fikentscher Verlag, n.d. [1937].

1937 (H) "A pók," trans. Thein Alfréd. In *Mai japán dekameron,* ed. Thein Alfréd, 249-61. Budapest: Nyugat.

1957 (ENG) "The victim," trans. Ivan Morris. *Paris Review* 16 (Spring-Summer): 13-20. Reprinted as "Tattoo," in *Modern Japanese Stories*, ed. Ivan Morris, 92-100. London: Spottiswoode, 1961.

1960 (D) "Tätowierung," trans. Kakuji Watanabe, revised by Heinrich Schmidt-Barrien. In *Japanische Meister der Erzählung*, ed. Kakuji Watanabe, 143-51. Bremen: Dorn.

1961 (ENG) "Tattoo," trans. Ryōzō Matsumoto. In *Japanese Literature, New and Old*, 105-18. Tokyo: The Hokuseido Press.

1961 (ENG) "Tattoo," trans. Ivan Morris. In *Modern Japanese Stories*, ed. Ivan Morris, 92-100. London: Spottiswoode. A reprint of "The victim" (1957).

1962 (P) "Tatuagem," trans. Konosuke Oseki. In *Maravilhas do conto japonês*, 83-90. São Paulo: Editora Cultrix.

1963 (ENG) "The Tattooer," trans. Howard Hibbett. In Junichiro Tanizaki, *Seven Japanese Tales*, 160-69. New York: Alfred A. Knopf. First published in *Show* 3 (May 1963): 70, 106-7.

1963 (F) "Le tatouage," trans. Marc Mécréant. *La Nouvelle Revue française* 125 (May): 817-29. Reprinted in *Anthologie du fantastique* 2, ed. Roger Caillois. Paris: Gallimard, coll. "Blanche." Reprinted in Tanizaki, *Œuvres* 1, 3-11. Paris: Gallimard.

1964 (NL) "Tatoeage," trans. Jef Last. In *Meesters der Japanse vertelkunst*, 142-50. Amsterdam: Meulenhoff. Reprinted in *Japans Verhaal*, 135-42. Amsterdam: Meulenhoff, 1983. Reprinted in *De Japanse Herfst: Moderne Japanese Verhalen*, 117-28. Amsterdam: Meulenhof, 1989.

1965 (I) "Il tatuaggio," trans. Atsuko Ricca Suga. In *Narratori giapponesi moderni,* ed. Atsuko Ricca Suga, 227-38. Milano: Bompiani.

1965 (D) *"Das Opfer," trans. Monique Humbert. In *Nippon: Moderne Erzählungen aus Japan von Mori Ogai bis Mishima Yukio*, 105-15. Zürich: Diogenes.

1965 (ESP) "Tatuo," trans. Teruhiko Isiguro. In *El Japana literaturo*, 223-30. Tokyo: Japana Esperanto Instituto.

1966 (SF) *"Tatuoija," trans. Kai Kaila. In Tanizaki Junichirō, *Unien silta*, 140-48. Helsinki: Tammi.

1967 (H) "Tetoválás," trans. Holti Mária. In *Modern japán elbeszélők*, 32-38. Budapest: Európa.

1968 (E) *"El tatuador," trans. Ángel Crespo. In Junichiro Tanizaki, *Cuentos crueles*, 167-76. Barcelona: Seix Barral.

1969 (D) "Tätowierung," trans. Heinz Brasch. In *Japan erzählt,* ed. Margarete Donath, 32-39. Hamburg: Fischer. A reprint of the 1937 edition of "Irezumi," revised by M. Donath. Reprinted in *Japan erzählt*: *Erzahlungen*, ed. Margarete Donath and Diana Donath, 11-20. Frankfurt: Fischer Taschenbuch Verlag, 1990.

1973 (SC) "Majstor tetoviranja," trans. Dragan Milenkovic. *Vestina sencenja*, 69-76.

1982 (F) "Le Tatouage," trans. Madeleine Lévy. *Le Promeneur* 5: 2-6.

1982 (BG) "Tatuirovkata," trans. Vera Vutova. In Tanizaki Jun'ichirō, *Portret na Shunkin*, 122-33. Sofia: Narodna Kultura.

1983 (CZ) "Tetování," trans. Vlasta Winkelhöferová. In Džuničiró Tanizaki, *Most snů*, 7-14. Praha: Vyšehrad.

1985 (I) "Il tatuaggio," trans. Adriana Boscaro. In Tanizaki Jun'ichirō, *Pianto di sirena e altri racconti*, 7-15. Milano: Feltrinelli. Reprinted in Tanizaki, *Opere,* 1-11. Milano: Bompiani, 1988.

1990 (D) "Die Tätowierung," trans. Siegfried Schaarschmidt. In *Das grosse Japan-Lesenbuch,* ed. Siegfried Schaarschmidt, 13-22. München: Goldmann.

"Shōnen" 少年 (1911)

1968 (ESP) "Knaboj," trans. Masao Miyamoto. In Junichiro Tanizaki, *El la vivo de Syunkin*, 47-78. Osaka: Librajo Pirato.

1988 (I) "Adolescenti," trans. Luisa Bienati. In Tanizaki, *Opere*, 29-61. Milano: Bompiani. First published in *Il Giappone* 25 ([1985] 1987): 105-38. Reprinted in Junichiro Tanizaki, *Il ponte dei sogni e altri racconti*, 3-38. Milano: Bompiani, 1995.

1997 (F) "Les Jeunes Garçons," trans. Cécile Sakai. In Tanizaki, *Œuvres* 1, 27-59. Paris: Gallimard.

*Shōshō Shigemoto no haha* 少將滋幹の母 (1950)

1966 (I) *La madre del generale Shigemoto*, trans. Guglielmo Scalise. Milano: Mondadori.

1976-78 (F) *La mère du capitaine palatin Shigemoto*, trans. Paul Anouilh. *Bulletin de l'Association des Français du Japon* (Tokyo, Maison franco-japonaise), 1-9.

1994 (ENG) *Captain Shigemoto's Mother*, trans. Anthony H. Chambers. In *Two Novellas by Junichirō Tanizaki—The Reed Cutter and Captain Shigemoto's Mother*, 55-180. New York: Alfred A. Knopf.

1998 (F) *La mère du général Shigemoto*, trans. Jacqueline Pigeot. In Tanizaki, *Œuvres* 2, 695-804. Paris: Gallimard.

*Shunkinshō* 春琴抄 (1933)

1936 (ENG) *The Story of Shunkin*, trans. Roy Humpherson and Hajime Okita. In Tanizaki Junichirō, *Ashikari and The Story of Shunkin*, 71-169. Tokyo: Hokuseido.

1960 (F) *L'histoire de Shunkin*, trans. Kikou Yamata. In Junichiro Tanizaki, *Deux amours cruelles*, 11-90. Paris: Stock.

1960 (D) *Biographie der Frühlingsharfe*, trans. Walter Donat and P. Y. Kawai. In *Die fünfstöckige Pagode,* ed. Walter Donat and P. Y. Kawai, 207-56. Düsseldorf: Diederichs.

1963 (I) *La storia di Shunkin*, trans. Giuseppe Ricca and Atsuko Ricca Suga. In Junichirō Tanizaki, *Due amori crudeli*, 5-96. Milano: Bompiani. Reprinted in Tanizaki, *Opere,* 599-669. Milano: Bompiani, 1988. Reprinted in Junichiro Tanizaki, *Il ponte dei sogni e altri racconti*, 89-164. Milano: Bompiani, 1995.

1963 (ENG) *A Portrait of Shunkin*, trans. Howard Hibbett. In Junichiro Tanizaki, *Seven Japanese Tales*, 3-84. New York: Alfred A. Knopf. Reprinted in Tanizaki Junichiro, *A Portrait of Shunkin* (with parallel translation), ed. Hiroshi Hayakawa. Tokyo: Hara Shobō, 1965.

1966 (SF) **Shunkin*, trans. Kai Kaila. In Tanizaki Junichirō, *Unien silta*, 7-76. Helsinki: Tammi.

1968 (E) **La historia de Shunkin*, trans. Jesús López Pacheco. In Junichiro Tanizaki, *Cuentos crueles*, 7-64. Barcelona: Seix Barral.

1968 (ESP) *El la vivo de Syunkin*, trans. Masao Miyamoto and Isiguro Teruhiko. In Tanizaki Junichiro, *El la vivo de Syunkin,* 79-139. Osaka: Librajo Pirato.

1969 (CZ) *Pokus o životopis Šunkin*, trans. Libuše Boháčková. In *Pět japonských novel*, 149-208. Praha: Odeon.

1971 (PL) *Shunkinshō, czyli rozmyślania nad życiem Wiosennej Harfy*, trans. Mikołaj Melanowicz. In Tanizaki Junichirō, *Dwie opowiesci o miłości okrutnej*, 77-177. Warszawa: Państwowy Instytut Wydawniczy.

1982 (BG) *Portret na Shunkin*, trans. Vera Vutova. In Tanizaki Jun'ichirō, *Portret na Shunkin*, 13-94. Sofia: Narodna Kultura.

1997 (F) *Shunkin, esquisse d'un portrait*, trans. Jean-Jacques Tschudin. In Tanizaki, *Œuvres* 1, 1393-467. Paris: Gallimard.

"Shunkinshō kōgo" 春琴抄後語 (1934)

1980 (ENG) "Postscript to 'A Portrait of Shunkin'," trans. Anthony H. Chambers. *Monumenta Nipponica* 35.4: 461-66.

1997 (F) "Postface." In *Shunkin, esquisse d'un portrait*, trans. Jean-Jacques Tschudin. In Tanizaki, *Œuvres* 1, 1393-467. Paris: Gallimard.

*Suterareru made* 捨てられる迄 (1914)

1994 (I) *Fino ad essere abbandonato*, trans. Emanuele Ciccarella. In Jun'ichirō Tanizaki, *Il veleno di Afrodite*, 7-88. Milano: Garzanti.

*Tade kuu mushi* 蓼喰ふ蟲 (1929)

1955 (ENG) *Some Prefer Nettles*, trans. Edward Seidensticker. New York: Knopf.

1955 (S) **Somliga tycker om nässlor*, trans. Nils Fredricson. Stockholm: Wahlström & Widstrand.

1957 (D) **Insel der Puppen*, trans. Curt Meyer-Clason. Esslingen: Bechtle.

1959 (F) *Le goût des orties*, trans. Sylvie Regnault-Gatier and Kazuo Anzai. Paris: Gallimard. Reprinted in Tanizaki, *Œuvres* 1, 941-1067. Paris: Gallimard, 1997.

1959 (SF) *Kukin makunsa mukaan*, trans. Yrjö Kivimies. Helsinki: Tammi.

1960 (I) *Gli insetti preferiscono le ortiche*, trans. Mario Teti. Milano: Mondadori.

1963 (E) **Hay quien prefiere las ortigas*, trans. María Luisa Borrás. Barcelona: Seix Barral.

1964 (NL) *Liever nog op de blaren*, trans. M. Coutinho. Amsterdam: De Bezige Bij, 1964. Reprinted Amsterdam: Meulenhoff, 1986.

1965 (CZ) *Ti, kteří raději kopřivy*, trans. Vlasta Hilská. Praha: Státní nakladatelství krásné literatury a umění.

1972 (PL) *Niektórzy wolą pokrzywy*, trans. Mikołaj Melanowicz. In Tanizaki Jun'ichirō, *Dziennik szalonego starca: Niektórzy wolą pokrzywy*, 157-304. Warszawa: Państwowy Instytut Wydawniczy.

1986 (H) *Aki a keserűfüvet szereti*, trans. Kolozsvári Papp László. Budapest: Európa.

"Tojō" 途上 (1920)

1991 (F) "Chemin faisant," trans. Marc Mécréant. In Junichirô Tanizaki, *L'affaire du "Yanagiyu" et autres récits étranges*, 225-79. Paris: Gallimard.

*Tomoda to Matsunaga no hanashi* 友田と松永の話 (1926)

1994 (I) *Storia di Tomoda e Matsunaga*, trans. Elisabetta Procchieschi, ed. Adriana Boscaro. Venezia: Marsilio.

1997 (F) *Histoire de Tomoda et Matsunaga*, trans. Anne Bayard-Sakai. In Tanizaki, *Œuvres* 1, 857-922. Paris: Gallimard.

"Watakushi" 私 (1921)

1963 (ENG) "The Thief," trans. Howard Hibbett. In Junichiro Tanizaki, *Seven Japanese Tales*, 170-85. New York: Alfred A. Knopf. Reprinted in *Murder in Japan: Japanese Stories of Crime and Detection*, ed. John L. Apostolou and Martin H. Greenberg, 72-84. New York: Dembner Books.

1966 (SF) *"Varas," trans. Kai Kaila. In Tanizaki Junichirō, *Unien silta*, 149-62. Helsinki: Tammi.

1968 (E) *"El ladrón," trans. Ángel Crespo. In Junichiro Tanizaki, *Cuentos crueles*, 177-91. Barcelona: Seix Barral.

1982 (BG) "Az," trans. Vera Vutova. In Tanizaki Jun'ichirō, *Portret na Shunkin*, 105-21. Sofia: Narodna Kultura.

1983 (NL) *"De Dief," trans. Jan Willem van de Wetering. In *Brief uit het dodenrijk*, ed. Jan W. van de Wetering, 27-37. Amsterdam: Loeb.

1985 (D) "Ich," trans. Reiko Sato and Ingrid Schuster. In *Japanische Kriminalgeschichten*, ed. Ingrid Schuster, 45-61. Stuttgart: Reclam.

1992 (D) *"Der Dieb," trans. Jürgen Bürger. In *Drachen und tote Gesichter: Japanische Kriminalstories 1*, ed. Janwillem van de Wetering, 13-28. Reinbek bei Hamburg: Rowohlt (rororo thriller 3036).

"Yanagiyu no jiken" 柳湯の事件 (1918)

1991 (F) "L'affaire du 'Yanagiyu'," trans. Marc Mécréant. In Junichirô Tanizaki, *L'affaire du "Yanagiyu" et autres récits étranges*, 9-35. Paris: Gallimard.

1997 (ENG) "The Incident at the Willow Bath House," trans. Phyllis I. Lyons. In *Studies in Modern Japanese Literature: Essays and Translations in Honor of Edwin McClellan*, ed. Dennis Washburn and Alan Tansman, 321-39. Michigan Monograph Series in Japanese Studies 20. Ann Arbor: Center for Japanese Studies, The University of Michigan.

*Yoshino kuzu* 吉野葛 (1931)

1982 (ENG) *Arrowoot*, trans. Anthony H. Chambers. In *Two Novellas by Junichirō Tanizaki—The Secret History of the Lord of Musashi* and *Arrowroot*, 143-99. New York: Alfred A. Knopf.

1984 (E) **Arrurruz*, trans. Néstor Dietrich. In Tanizaki Junichirō, *La historia secreta del señor de Musashi/Arrurruz*. Buenos Aires: Ed. Sudamericana.

1987 (F) *Le lierre de Yoshino*, trans. René de Ceccatty and Ryôji Nakamura. In Junichirô Tanizaki, *La vie secrète du seigneur de Musashi, suivi de Le lierre de Yoshino*, 157-211. Paris: Gallimard.

1989 (E) *Enredadera de Yoshino*, trans. Fernando Rodríguez-Izquierdo. In Tanizaki Junichiroo, *La vida enmascarada del señor de Musashi/Enredadera de Yoshino*. Barcelona: Editorial Edhasa.

1997 (F) *Yoshino*, trans. Jacqueline Pigeot. In Tanizaki, *Œuvres* 1, 1069-123. Paris: Gallimard.

1998 (I) *Yoshino*, trans. Adriana Boscaro. Venezia: Marsilio.

*Yōshō jidai* 幼少時代 (1955)

1988 (ENG) *Childhood Years—A Memoir*, trans. Paul McCarthy. Tokyo: Kodansha International.

1993 (F) *Années d'enfance*, trans. Marc Mécréant. Paris: Gallimard, 1993. Reprinted in Tanizaki, *Œuvres* 2, 805-1017. Paris: Gallimard, 1998.

1997 (NL) *Kinderjaren: Herinneringen*, trans. Tinke Davids. Amsterdam: De Arbeiderspers.

"Yume no ukihashi" 夢の浮橋 (1959)

1963 (ENG) "The Bridge of Dreams," trans. Howard Hibbett. In Junichiro Tanizaki, *Seven Japanese Tales*, 95-159. New York: Alfred A. Knopf. Reprinted in *Contemporary Japanese Literature: An Anthology of Fiction, Film, and Other Writing Since 1945*, ed. Howard Hibbett, 354-88. Tokyo: Tuttle, 1978.

1965 (I) "Il ponte dei sogni," trans. Atsuko Ricca Suga. In *Narratori giapponesi moderni*, ed. Atsuko Ricca Suga, 239-92. Milano: Bompiani. Reprinted in Tanizaki, *Opere*, 931-87. Milano: Bompiani, 1988. Reprinted in Junichiro Tanizaki, *Il ponte dei sogni e altri racconti*, 165-226. Milano: Bompiani, 1995.

1966 (SF) *"Unien silta," trans. Kai Kaila. In Tanizaki Junichirō, *Unien silta*, 85-139. Helsinki: Tammi.

1968 (E) *"El puente de los sueños," trans. Ángel Crespo. In Junichiro Tanizaki, *Cuentos crueles*, 111-65. Barcelona: Seix Barral.

1973 (H) "Az álmok hídja," trans. Pál Félix. *Nagyvilág* 11: 1615-43.

1979 (D) *"Die Traumbrücke," trans. Reinhild Böhnke. In Tanizaki Junichiro, *Die Traumbrücke*, 5-57. Berlin: Volk und Welt.

1982 (PL) "Ulotny most snów," trans. Mikołaj Melanowicz. *Literatura na Świecie* 1: 100-67. Reprinted in *Tydzień świętego mozołu*, 411-65. Warszawa: Państwowy Instytut Wydawniczy.

1983 (CZ) "Most snů," trans. Vlasta Winkelhöferová. In Džuničiró Tanizaki, *Most snů*, 81-128. Praha: Vyšehrad.

1998 (F) "Le Pont flottant des songes," trans. Jean-Jacques Tschudin. In Tanizaki, *Œuvres* 2, 1199-256. Paris: Gallimard.

"Zangyakuki" 殘虐記 (1958)

1998 (F) "Chronique inhumaine," trans. Marc Mécréant. In Tanizaki, *Œuvres* 2, 1123-98. Paris: Gallimard.

"Zoku akuma" 続悪魔 (1913)

1986 (I) "Il demone" (Seconda parte), trans. Lydia Origlia. In Jun'ichirō Tanizaki, *Il dramma stregato*, 31-65. Milano: SE.

"Zoku Radō sensei" 続蘿洞先生 (1928)

1990 (ENG) "Professor Rado," trans. Paul McCarthy. In Jun'ichiro Tanizaki, *A Cat, a Man, and Two Women*, 137-64. Tokyo: Kodansha International.

1994 (F) "Le professeur Radô revisité," trans. Jean-Jacques Tschudin. In Junichirô Tanizaki, *Le chat, son maître et ses deux maîtresses—Nouvelles*, 175-92. Paris: Gallimard. Reprinted in Tanizaki, *Œuvres* 2, 843-55. Paris: Gallimard, 1997.

"Zōnen" 憎念 (1914)

1997 (F) "La haine," trans. Anne Bayard-Sakai. In Tanizaki, *Œuvres* 1, 91-100. Paris: Gallimard.

Note.

Bibliographies of translations of Japanese works generally list also the following:

Tanizaki Jun'ichirō, "Kyoto, her nature, food . . . and women," *This Is Japan* 12 (1965): 222–25.

But they never give the original title nor the name of the translator. To my knowledge an original text in Japanese has never existed and it is highly possible that the short article is the result of an interview with Tanizaki, rehashed and adapted for a foreign reader by the interviewer or the editorial staff of *This Is Japan*. I am grateful to Professor Edward Seidensticker for this suggestion.

# 2

# Translations of Titles by Language (based on this bibliography)

**French [F] (54):**
*Aisureba koso*, “Aozukashi no hanashi,” “Aru shōnen no osore,” *Ashikari* (2), “A to B no hanashi,” *Bushūkō hiwa* (2), *Byakko no yu*, “Byōjoku no gensō,” “Chiisana ōkoku,” *Chijin no ai*, “Dokutan,” *Eien no gūzō*, “Fumiko no ashi,” “Futari no chigo” (2), *Fūten rōjin nikki* (2), “Haha o kouru ki,” “Hassan Kan no yōjutsu,” “Himitsu” (2), “Hitofusa no kami,” *In’ei raisan*, “Itansha no kanashimi,” “Jinmenso,” *Kagi* (2), “Kin to gin,” “Kirin,” “Konjiki no shi,” “Kyōfu,” “Kyōto o omou,” *Manji*, *Mōmoku monogatari* (2), *Mumyō to Aizen* (2), *Neko to Shōzō to futari no onna*, “Ningyo no nageki,” “Norowareta gikyoku,” *Okuni to Gohei*, *Otsuya koroshi*, “Radō sensei,” “Randa no setsu,” *Sasameyuki* (2), “Shisei” (3), “Shōnen,” *Shōshō Shigemoto no haha* (2), *Shunkinshō* (2), “Shunkinshō kōgo,” *Tade kuu mushi*, “Tojō,” *Tomoda to Matsunaga no hanashi*, “Yanagiyu no jiken,” *Yoshino kuzu* (2), “Yōshō jidai,” “Yume no ukihashi,” “Zangyakuki,” “Zoku Radō sensei,” “Zōnen.”

**Italian [I] (46):**
*Aisureba koso*, “Akuma,” *Amachua kurabu*, *Ashikari*, “Ave Maria,” *Bushūkō hiwa*, *Chijin no ai*, “Fumiko no ashi,” “Futari no chigo,” *Fūten rōjin nikki*, “Geidan,” “Haha o kouru ki,” *Hakuchūkigo*, “Himitsu,” “Hōkan,” “Hyōfū,” *In’ei raisan*, “Itansha no kanashimi,” *Jōtarō*, *Kagi*, “Ken’etsukan,” “Kirin,” “Konjiki no shi,” “Majutsushi,” *Manji*, *Mōmoku monogatari*, *Neko to Shōzō to futari no onna*, “Nihon ni okeru Kurippun jiken,” “Ningyo no nageki,” “Norowareta gikyoku,” *Otsuya koroshi*, “Randa no setsu,” “Ren’ai oyobi shikijō,” “Sakana no Ri Taihaku,” *Sasameyuki*, *Shinzei*, “Shisei” (2), “Shōnen,” *Shōshō Shigemoto no haha*, *Shunkinshō*, *Suterareru made*, *Tade kuu mushi*, *Tomoda to Matsunaga no hanashi*, *Yoshino kuzu*, “Yume no ukihashi,” “Zoku akuma.”

**English [ENG] (35):**
“Aoi hana,” *Ashikari* (2), *Bushūkō hiwa*, *Byakko no yu*, “Chiisana ōkoku,” *Chijin no ai*, *Fūten rōjin nikki*, “Haha o kouru ki” (2), “Himitsu,” “Hōkan,” *In’ei raisan*, *Kagi*, “Kyōfu,” *Mandorin o hiku otoko*, *Manji*, *Mōmoku monogatari*, *Neko to Shōzō to futari no onna* (2), *Okuni to Gohei* (2), *Otsuya koroshi*, “Radō sensei,” “Sakana no Ri Taihaku,” *Sasameyuki*, “Shanhai kōyūki,” *Shinzei*, “Shisei” (5), *Shōshō Shigemoto no haha*, *Shunkinshō* (2), “Shunkinshō kōgo,” *Tade kuu mushi*, “Watakushi,” “Yanagiyu no jiken,” *Yoshino kuzu*, “Yōshō jidai,” “Yume no ukihashi,” “Zoku Radō sensei.”

**German [D] (16):**
"Aoi hana," *Bushūkō hiwa*, "Chiisana ōkoku," *Chijin no ai*, *Fūten rōjin nikki*, *In'ei raisan*, *Kagi*, "Kozō no yume," *Mōmoku monogatari*, *Neko to Shōzō to futari no onna*, *Sasameyuki*, "Shisei" (5), *Shunkinshō*, *Tade kuu mushi*, "Watakushi" (2), "Yume no ukihashi."

**Spanish [E] (14):**
*Aisureba koso*, "Aoi hana," *Ashikari*, *Bushūkō hiwa* (2), *In'ei raisan*, "Kyōfu," *Mōmoku monogatari*, *Sasameyuki*, "Shisei," *Shunkinshō*, *Tade kuu mushi*, "Watakushi," *Yoshino kuzu* (2), "Yume no ukihashi."

**Czech [CZ] (11):**
*Ashikari*, *Fūten rōjin nikki*, "Haha o kouru ki," *In'ei raisan*, *Mōmoku monogatari*, *Otsuya koroshi*, *Sasameyuki*, "Shisei," *Shunkinshō*, *Tade kuu mushi*, "Yume no ukihashi."

**Dutch [NL] (10):**
*Bushūkō hiwa*, *Fūten rōjin nikki*, *In'ei raisan*, *Kagi*, *Manji*, *Sasameyuki*, "Shisei," *Tade kuu mushi*, "Watakushi," *Yōshō jidai*.

**Finnish [SF] (10):**
"Aoi hana," *Kagi*, "Kyōfu," *Mōmoku monogatari*, *Sasameyuki*, "Shisei," *Shunkinshō*, *Tade kuu mushi*, "Watakushi," "Yume no ukihashi."

**Bulgarian [BG] (7):**
"Hōkan," *Kagi*, "Kyakugirai," "Kyōfu," "Shisei," *Shunkinshō*, "Watakushi."

**Polish [PL] (6):**
*Ashikari*, *Bushūkō hiwa*, *Fūten rōjin nikki*, *Shunkinshō*, *Tade kuu mushi*, "Yume no ukihashi."

**Esperanto [ESP] (5):**
*Mumyō to Aizen*, *Okuni to Gohei*, "Shisei," "Shōnen," *Shunkinshō*.

**Hungarian [H] (5):**
*Fūten rōjin nikki*, *Kagi*, "Shisei" (2), *Tade kuu mushi*, "Yume no ukihashi."

**Serbo-croatian [SC] (3):**
*Kagi*, *Sasameyuki*, "Shisei."

**Portuguese [P] (2):**
*Chijin no ai*, "Shisei."

**Swedish [S] (2):**
*Kagi*, *Tade kuu mushi*.

**Danish [DK] (1):**
*Kagi*.

**Slovenian [SL] (1):**
*Sasameyuki*.

# 3

# Translations in Chronological Order

| | |
|---|---|
| 1917 | "Shisei" (ENG) |
| 1921-22 | "Sakana no Ri Taihaku" (ENG) |
| 1923 | "Shisei" (ENG) |
| 1924 | *Okuni to Gohei* (ENG)<br>*Shinzei* (ENG)<br>"Shisei" (F) |
| 1925 | *Aisureba koso* (F)<br>*Eien no gūzō* (F)<br>"Shisei" (D) |
| 1927 | "Himitsu" (F)<br>*Mumyō to Aizen* (F)<br>*Otsuya koroshi* (ENG) |
| 1929 | *Aisureba koso* (I) |
| 1930 | *Aisureba koso* (E)<br>*Byakko no yu* (ENG)<br>"Shisei" (D) |
| 1931 | *Okuni to Gohei* (ENG) |
| 1935-36 | *Mōmoku monogatari* (F) |
| 1936 | *Ashikari* (ENG)<br>*Shunkinshō* (ENG) |
| 1937 | "Shisei" (H) |
| 1940 | "Futari no chigo" (F) |

1942 *Otsuya koroshi* (CZ)

1951 "Haha o kouru ki" (ENG)

1955 *Tade kuu mushi* (ENG)
*Tade kuu mushi* (S)

1957 *Sasameyuki* (ENG)
"Shisei" (ENG)
*Tade kuu mushi* (D)

1959 *Tade kuu mushi* (F)
*Tade kuu mushi* (SF)

1960 *Ashikari* (F)
*Kagi* (ENG)
"Shisei" (D)
*Shunkinshō* (F)
*Shunkinshō* (D)
*Tade kuu mushi* (I)

1961 *Kagi* (D)
*Kagi* (SF)
*Sasameyuki* (I)
"Shisei" (ENG)

1962 *Kagi* (DK)
*Kagi* (S)
*Kagi* (NL)
"Shisei" (P)

1963 "Aoi hana" (ENG)
*Ashikari* (I)
*Kagi* (I)
*Kagi* (F)
"Kyōfu" (ENG)
*Mōmoku monogatari* (ENG)
"Shisei" (ENG)
"Shisei" (F)
*Shunkinshō* (I)
*Shunkinshō* (ENG)
*Tade kuu mushi* (E)
"Watakushi" (ENG)
"Yume no ukihashi" (ENG)

1964 *Sasameyuki* (D)
*Sasameyuki* (F)
"Shisei" (NL)
*Tade kuu mushi* (NL)

1965 *Fūten rōjin nikki* (I)
*Fūten rōjin nikki* (ENG)
"Shisei" (D)
"Shisei" (I)
"Shisei" (ESP)
*Tade kuu mushi* (CZ)
"Yume no ukihashi" (I)

1966 "Aoi hana" (SF)
*Fūten rōjin nikki* (D)
"Hōkan" (ENG)
"Kyōfu" (SF)
*Mōmoku monogatari* (SF)
*Sasameyuki* (E)
"Shisei" (SF)
*Shōshō Shigemoto no haha* (I)
*Shunkinshō* (SF)
"Watakushi" (SF)
"Yume no ukihashi" (SF)

1967 *Chijin no ai* (I)
*Fūten rōjin nikki* (F)
*Sasameyuki* (SL)
"Shisei" (H)

1968 *Ashikari* (E)
*Fūten rōjin nikki* (NL)
"Kyōfu" (E)
*Mōmoku monogatari* (E)
*Mumyō to Aizen* (ESP)
*Okuni to Gohei* (ESP)
"Shisei" (E)
"Shōnen" (ESP)
*Shunkinshō* (E)
*Shunkinshō* (ESP)
"Watakushi" (E)
"Yume no ukihashi" (E)

1969 *Kagi* (SC)
"Shisei" (D)
*Shunkinshō* (CZ)

1970 *Bushūkō hiwa* (I)
*Chijin no ai* (D)
*Mōmoku monogatari* (I)
*Neko to Shōzō to futari no onna* (I)

1971 *Ashikari* (PL)
*Shunkinshō* (PL)

| | |
|---|---|
| 1972 | *Fūten rōjin nikki* (PL) |
| | *Mandorin o hiku otoko* (ENG) |
| | *Sasameyuki* (SC) |
| | *Tade kuu mushi* (PL) |
| 1973 | "Shisei" (SC) |
| | "Yume no ukihashi" (H) |
| 1975 | "Chiisana ōkoku" (D) |
| 1976-78 | *Shōshō Shigemoto no haha* (F) |
| 1977 | *In'ei raisan* (ENG) |
| | *In'ei raisan* (F) |
| | *Sasameyuki* (CZ) |
| 1979 | *Mōmoku monogatari* (D) |
| | "Yume no ukihashi" (D) |
| 1980 | *Fūten rōjin nikki* (H) |
| | "Haha o kouru ki" (ENG) |
| | "Shunkinshō kōgo" (ENG) |
| 1982 | *Bushūkō hiwa* (ENG) |
| | "Hōkan" (BG) |
| | *In'ei raisan* (I) |
| | "Kyakugirai" (BG) |
| | "Kyōfu" (BG) |
| | *Manji* (I) |
| | "Shisei" (F) |
| | "Shisei" (BG) |
| | *Shunkinshō* (BG) |
| | "Watakushi" (BG) |
| | *Yoshino kuzu* (ENG) |
| | "Yume no ukihashi" (PL) |
| 1983 | *Ashikari* (CZ) |
| | "Haha o kouru ki" (CZ) |
| | *Mōmoku monogatari* (CZ) |
| | "Shisei" (CZ) |
| | "Watakushi" (NL) |
| | "Yume no ukihashi" (CZ) |
| 1984 | *Bushūkō hiwa* (E) |
| | *Yoshino kuzu* (E) |
| 1985 | *Chijin no ai* (ENG) |
| | "Himitsu" (I) |
| | "Hōkan" (I) |
| | "Kirin" (I) |
| | "Majutsushi" (I) |

| | |
|---|---|
| | *Manji* (F) |
| | "Ningyo no nageki" (I) |
| | "Shisei" (I) |
| | "Watakushi" (D) |
| 1986 | "Akuma" (I) |
| | *Bushūkō hiwa* (NL) |
| | *Chijin no ai* (P) |
| | "Fumiko no ashi" (F) |
| | "Kirin" (F) |
| | "Norowareta gikyoku" (I) |
| | *Otsuya koroshi* (I) |
| | *Tade kuu mushi* (H) |
| | "Zoku akuma" (I) |
| 1987 | *Bushūkō hiwa* (F) |
| | *In'ei raisan* (D) |
| | *Yoshino kuzu* (F) |
| 1988 | *Chijin no ai* (F) |
| | *Neko to Shōzō to futari no onna* (ENG) |
| | "Shōnen" (I) |
| | *Yōshō jidai* (ENG) |
| 1989 | *Bushūkō hiwa* (E) |
| | *Manji* (NL) |
| | *Yoshino kuzu* (E) |
| 1990 | "Chiisana ōkoku" (ENG) |
| | *Kagi* (H) |
| | *Neko to Shōzō to futari no onna* (ENG) |
| | "Radō sensei" (ENG) |
| | "Shisei" (D) |
| | "Zoku Radō sensei" (ENG) |
| 1991 | "Aozukashi no hanashi" (F) |
| | "Hassan Kan no yōjutsu" (F) |
| | "Jinmenso" (F) |
| | "Kin to gin" (F) |
| | "Norowareta gikyoku" (F) |
| | *Sasameyuki* (SF) |
| | "Tojō" (F) |
| | "Yanagiyu no jiken" (F) |
| 1992 | "Watakushi" (D) |
| 1993 | "Himitsu" (ENG) |
| | *Yōshō jidai* (F) |
| 1994 | "Aoi hana" (E) |

"Aoi hana" (D)
*Ashikari* (ENG)
*Bushūkō hiwa* (D)
"Chiisana ōkoku" (F)
*Hakuchūkigo* (I)
*In'ei raisan* (E)
*In'ei raisan* (NL)
*Jōtarō* (I)
*Kagi* (BG)
"Kozō no yume" (D)
*Manji* (ENG)
*Neko to Shōzō to futari no onna* (F)
"Radō sensei" (F)
*Sasameyuki* (NL)
*Shōshō Shigemoto no haha* (ENG)
*Suterareru made* (I)
*Tomoda to Matsunaga no hanashi* (I)
"Zoku Radō sensei" (F)

1995 *Amachua kurabu* (I)
"Ave Maria" (I)
"Fumiko no ashi" (I)
"Geidan" (I)
"Hyōfū" (I)
"Ken'etsukan" (I)
"Konjiki no shi" (I)
"Nihon ni okeru Kurippun jiken" (I)
"Randa no setsu" (I)
"Ren'ai oyobi shikijō" (I)
"Sakana no Ri Taihaku" (I)
*Shinzei* (I)

1996 *Bushūkō hiwa* (PL)
*Neko to Shōzō to futari no onna* (D)
"Randa no setsu" (F)

1997 "A to B no hanashi" (F)
"Aru shōnen no osore" (F)
*Ashikari* (F)
*Bushūkō hiwa* (F)
*Byakko no yu* (F)
"Byōjoku no gensō" (F)
"Dokutan" (F)
"Futari no chigo" (F)
"Haha o kouru ki" (F)
"Himitsu" (F)
"Hitofusa no kami" (F)
"Itansha no kanashimi" (F)
"Kirin" (F)

"Konjiki no shi" (F)
"Kyōfu" (F)
"Kyōto o omou" (F)
*Mōmoku monogatari* (F)
*Mumyō to Aizen* (F)
"Ningyo no nageki" (F)
*Okuni to Gohei* (F)
*Otsuya koroshi* (F)
"Shanhai kōyūki" (ENG)
"Shōnen" (F)
*Shunkinshō* (F)
"Shunkinshō kōgo" (F)
*Tomoda to Matsunaga no hanashi* (F)
"Yanagiyu no jiken" (ENG)
*Yoshino kuzu* (F)
*Yōshō jidai* (NL)
"Zōnen" (F)

1998 *Fūten rōjin nikki* (F)
*Fūten rōjin nikki* (CZ)
*In'ei raisan* (CZ)
*Kagi* (F)
*Sasameyuki* (F)
*Shōshō Shigemoto no haha* (F)
*Yoshino kuzu* (I)
"Yume no ukihashi" (F)
"Zangyakuki" (F)

1999 "Futari no chigo" (I)
"Haha o kouru ki" (I)
"Itansha no kanashimi" (I)

# 4

# Contents of Collections

This list comprises collections of translations of Tanizaki. Some are reprints of pieces taken from different books or previously published separately.
If the contents of a collection are fully indicated by its title (e.g. *The Secret History of the Lord of Musashi and Arrowroot*), the collection is not included here.
Works are arranged in alphabetical order by title, including all title words (*a*, *die*, *el*, *il*, *the*, etc.).
The names of translators are omitted here, but they can be found under the original Japanese titles in Section 1. Where known, the name of the compiler (writer/author) of introductions, notes, and prefaces is given.

*A Cat, a Man and Two Women*. Tokyo and New York: Kodansha International, 1990
*A Cat, a Man and Two Women* (*Neko to Shōzō to futari no onna*, 1-99), *The Little Kingdom* ("Chiisana ōkoku," 101-35), "Professor Rado" ("Radō sensei," 137-64).
Preface (Paul McCarthy), vii-xiv.

*Cuentos crueles*. Barcelona: Seix Barral, 1968
*La historia de Shunkin* (*Shunkinshō*, 7-64), *Ashikari* (*Ashikari*, 65-99), "Terror" ("Kyōfu," 101-10), "El puente de los sueños" ("Yume no ukihashi," 111-65), "El tatuador" ("Shisei," 167-76), "El ladrón" ("Watakushi," 177-91), *Un cuento de ciego* (*Mōmoku monogatari*, 193-272).

*Deux amours cruelles*. Paris: Stock, 1960
*L'histoire de Shunkin* (*Shunkinshō*, 11-90), *Ashikari; un couple dans les roseaux* (*Ashikari*, 91-139).
Préface (Henry Miller), 7-10.

*Die Traumbrücke*. Berlin: Volk und Welt, 1979
"Die Traumbrücke" ("Yume no ukihashi," 5-57), *Die Erzählung eines Blinden* (*Mōmoku monogatari*, 59-135).

*Divagazioni sull'otium e altri scritti*. Venezia: Cafoscarina, 1995
*Shinzei* (*Shinzei*, 19-31), "Turbine" ("Hyōfū," 33-67), "Li Bo, il pesce" ("Sakana no Ri Taihaku," 69-79), "Il censore" ("Ken'etsukan," 81-111), *Amateur Club* (*Amachua kurabu*, 113-57), "Un 'caso Crippen' giapponese" ("Nihon ni okeru Kurippun jiken," 159-73), "Divagazioni sull'otium"

("Randa no setsu," 175-92), "Amore e passione" ("Ren'ai oyobi shikijō," 193-227), "Geidan" ("Chiacchierata sull'arte," 229-76).
Preface: "Un omaggio al 'grande vecchio'" (Adriana Boscaro), 9-18.

*Due amori crudeli*. Milano: Bompiani, 1963
*Storia di Shunkin* (*Shunkinshō*, 5-96), *I canneti* (*Ashikari*, 97-157).

*Dwie opowieści o miłości okrutnej*. Warszawa: Państwowy Instytut Wydawniczy, 1971
*Ashikari, czyli źle mi bez ciebie* (*Ashikari*, 7-75), *Shunkinshō, czyli rozmyślania nad życiem Wiosennej Harfy* (*Shunkinshō*, 77-177).

*El la vivo de Syunkin*. Osaka: Librejo Pirato, 1968
*Okuni kaj Gohei* (*Okuni to Gohei*, 7-24), *Mumyô kaj Aizen* (*Mumyō to Aizen*, 25-46), "Knaboj" ("Shōnen," 47-78), *El la vivo de Syunkin* (*Shunkinshō*, 79-139).

*Il dramma stregato*. Milano: SE, 1986
"Il demone" (Prima parte) ("Akuma," 9-30), "Il demone" (Seconda parte) ("Zoku Akuma," 31-65), *L'assassinio di O-Tsuya* (*Otsuya koroshi*, 67-121), "Il dramma stregato" ("Norowareta gikyoku," 123-60).
Afterword: *Jun'ichirō Tanizaki* (Mishima Yukio), 161-66.

*Il ponte dei sogni e altri racconti*. Milano: Bompiani, 1995
"Adolescenti" ("Shōnen," 5-38), *I canneti* (*Ashikari*, 39-88), *La storia di Shunkin* (*Shunkinshō*, 91-164), "Il ponte dei sogni" ("Yume no ukihashi," 165-226).
Biobibliographical note (Adriana Boscaro), v-xii.

*Il veleno di Afrodite—Due racconti*. Milano: Garzanti, 1994
*Fino ad essere abbandonato* (*Suterareru made*, 7-88), *Jōtarō* (*Jōtarō*, 89-177).
Afterword (Emanuele Ciccarella), 179-96.

*L'affaire du "Yanagiyu" et autres récits étranges*. Paris: Gallimard, 1991
"L'affaire du 'Yanagiyu'" ("Yanagiyu no jiken," 9-35), "La tumeur à face humaine" ("Jinmenso," 37-62), "L'or et l'argent" ("Kin to gin," 63-154), "Un drame maudit" ("Norowareta gikyoku," 155-205), "Hassan Khan le magicien" ("Hassan Kan no yōjutsu," 207-54), "Chemin faisant" ("Tojō," 255-79), "Monsieur Aozuka" ("Aozukashi no hanashi," 281-325).

*Le chat, son maître et ses deux maîtresses—Nouvelles*. Paris: Gallimard, 1994
*Le chat, son maître et ses deux maîtresses* (*Neko to Shōzō to futari no onna*, 9-115), "Le petit royaume" ("Chiisana ōkoku," 117-56), "Le professeur Radô" ("Radō sensei," 157-73), "Le professeur Radô revisité" ("Zoku Radō sensei," 175-92).

*Most snů*. Praha: Vyšehrad, 1983
"Tetování" ("Shisei," 7-14), *Požaté rákosí* (*Ashikari*, 17-55), "O touze po matce" ("Haha o kouru ki," 59-77), "Most snů" ("Yume no ukihashi," 81-128), *Slepcův příběh* (*Mōmoku monogatari*, 131-201).
Afterword: "Ohlas tradičních japonských estetických idealů v prózách Džuničiróa Tanizakiho" (Vlasta Winkelhoferövá), 203-7.

*Mumyô et Aizen*. Tokyo: Hakusuisha, 1927
*Mumyô et Aizen* (*Mumyō to Aizen*, 1-75), *L'eternella* [sic] *idole* (*Eien no gūzō*, 77-181).

*Nostalgia della madre*. Milano, SE: 1999

"La tristezza di un eretico" ("Itansha no kanashimi," 11-65), "I due novizi" ("Futari no chigo," 67-95), "Nostalgia della madre" ("Haha o kouru ki," 97-120).

*Œuvres* 1. Paris: Gallimard, 1997

"Le tatouage" ("Shisei," 3-11), "Le Kilin" ("Kirin," 13-26), "Les jeunes garçons" ("Shōnen," 27-59), "Le secret" ("Himitsu," 61-81), "Terreur" ("Kyōfu," 83-90), "La haine" ("Zōnen," 91-100), "Une mort dorée" ("Konjiki no shi," 101-29), *Le meurtre d'O-Tsuya* (*Otsuya koroshi*, 131-96), "L'espion du Kaiser" ("Dokutan," 197-237), "Visions d'un lit de douleur" ("Byōjoku no gensō," 239-62), "La complainte de la sirène" ("Ningyo no nageki," 263-88), "Morosités d'un hérétique" ("Itansha no kanashimi," 289-352), "Les deux novices" ("Futari no chigo," 353-75), "Le petit royaume" ("Chiisana ōkoku," 377-405), "Nostalgie de ma mère" ("Haha o kouru ki," 407-30), "Le pied de Fumiko" ("Fumiko no ashi," 431-58), "Affres d'un jeune garçon" ("Aru shōnen no osore," 459-505), "Histoire de A et B" ("A to B no hanashi," 507-50), *O-Kuni et Gohei* (*Okuni to Gohei*, 551-71), *La source au renard blanc* (*Byakko no yu*, 573-96), *Un amour insensé* (*Chijin no ai*, 597-810), *Mumyô et Aizen* (*Mumyō to Aizen*, 811-30), "Le professeur Radô" ("Radō sensei," 831-42), "Le professeur Radô revisité" ("Zoku Radō sensei," 843-55), *Histoire de Tomoda et Matsunaga* (*Tomoda to Matsunaga no hanashi*, 857-922), "La mèche" ("Hitofusa no kami," 923-39), *Le goût des orties* (*Tade kuu mushi*, 941-1067), *Yoshino* (*Yoshino kuzu*, 1069-123), *Le récit de l'aveugle* (*Mōmoku monogatari*, 1125-206), *Histoire secrète du sire de Musashi* (*Bushūkō hiwa*, 1207-346), *Le coupeur de roseaux* (*Ashikari*, 1347-92), *Shunkin, esquisse d'un portrait* (*Shunkinshō*, 1393-467), *Éloge de l'ombre* (*In'ei raisan*, 1469-1512), *Le chat, son maître et ses deux maîtresses* (*Neko to Shōzō to futari no onna*, 1513-92).

Préface (Ninomiya Masayuki, xi-lii), Chronologie (Ninomiya Masayuki, liii-lxxi), Note sur la présente édition (Jacqueline Pigeot, lxxiii-lxxv), Notices et notes (1593-901), Notice sur l'œuvre théâtrale (Jean-Jacques Tschudin, 1903-15), Répertoire (1917-36), Cartes (1937-44).

*Œuvres* 2. Paris: Gallimard, 1998

*Bruine de neige* (*Sasameyuki*, 1-694), *La mère du général Shigemoto* (*Shōshō Shigemoto no haha*, 695-804), *Années d'enfance* (*Yōshō jidai*, 805-1017), *La clef* (*Kagi*, 1019-122), "Chronique inhumaine" ("Zangyakuki," 1123-98), "Le pont flottant des songes" ("Yume no ukihashi," 1199-256), *Journal d'un vieux fou* (*Fūten rōjin nikki*, 1257-387).

Préface (Ninomiya Masayuki, ix-xxxiv), Chronologie (Ninomiya Masayuki, xxxv-xli), Note sur la présente édition (Jean-Jacques Tschudin, xliii-xliv), Notices et notes (1389-582), Répertoire (1583-602), Bibliographie générale (Jean-Jacques Tschudin, 1603-8), Cartes (1609-15).

*Opere*. Milano: Bompiani, 1988

"Il tatuaggio" ("Shisei," 1-11), "Kirin" ("Kirin," 13-28), "Adolescenti" ("Shōnen," 29-61), "Buffone di professione" ("Hōkan," 63-79), "Il segreto" ("Himitsu," 81-103), "Pianto di sirena" ("Ningyo no nageki," 105-29), "Il prestigiatore" ("Majutsushi," 131-56), *L'amore di uno sciocco* (*Chijin no ai*, 157-400), *Vita segreta del signore di Bushū* (*Bushūkō hiwa*, 401-551), *I canneti* (*Ashikari*, 553-98), *La storia di Shunkin* (*Shunkinshō*, 599-669), *Libro d'ombra* (*In'ei raisan*, 671-726), *La gatta, Shōzō e le due donne* (*Neko to Shōzō to futari no onna*, 727-821), *La chiave* (*Kagi*, 823-929), "Il ponte dei sogni" ("Yume no ukihashi," 931-87), *Diario di un vecchio pazzo* (*Fūten rōjin nikki*, 989-1134).

Adriana Boscaro: Il grande vecchio, vii-xxxiv; Cronologia, xxxv-xlviii; Glossario, 1135-54; La fortuna di Tanizaki in Italia, 1155-68.

*Pianto di sirena e altri racconti*. Milano: Feltrinelli, 1985

"Il tatuaggio" ("Shisei," 7-15), "Kirin" ("Kirin," 16-29), "Buffone di professione" ("Hōkan," 30-44), "Il segreto" ("Himitsu," 45-65), "Pianto di sirena" ("Ningyo no nageki," 66-88), "Il prestigiatore" ("Majutsushi," 89-112).

Afterword: (Adriana Boscaro), 113-20.

*Portret na Shunkin*. Sofia: Narodna Kultura, 1982

*Portret na Shunkin* (*Shunkinshō*, 13-94), "Uzas" ("Kyōfu," 95-104), "Az" ("Watakushi," 105-21), "Tatuirovkata" ("Shisei," 122-33), "Komediantat" ("Hōkan," 134-54), "Samozivetzat" ("Kyakugirai," 155-67).

Introduction: "Vazhvala na syankata" (Tzvetana Kristeva), 5-12.

*Seven Japanese Tales*. New York: Alfred A. Knopf, 1963

*A Portrait of Shunkin* (*Shunkinshō*, 3-84), "Terror" ("Kyōfu," 85-94), "The Bridge of Dreams" ("Yume no ukihashi," 95-159, "The Tattooer" ("Shisei," 160-69), "The Thief" ("Watakushi," 170-85), "Aguri" ("Aoi hana," 186-204), *A Blind Man's Tale* (*Mōmoku monogatari*, 205-98).

Introduction (Howard Hibbett), iii-ix.

*Unien silta*. Helsinki: Tammi, 1966

*Shunkin* (*Shunkinshō*, 7-76), "Kauhu" ("Kyōfu," 77-84), "Unien silta" ("Yume no ukihashi," 85-139), "Tatuoija" ("Shisei," 140-48), "Varas" ("Watakushi," 149-62), "Aguri" ("Aoi hana," 163-79), *Sokean miehen kertomus* (*Mōmoku monogatari*, 180-256).

*Vita segreta del signore di Bushu*. Milano: Bompiani, 1970

*Vita segreta del signore di Bushu* (*Bushūkō hiwa*, 5-181), *Racconto d'un cieco* (*Mōmoku monogatari*, 183-286), *La gatta, Shozo e le due donne* (*Neko to Shōzō to futari no onna*, 287-389).

# 5

# Index of Translated Titles

Works are arranged by alphabetical order, including all title words.

"Chemin faisant" ("Tojō")
"Chiacchierata sull'arte" ("Geidan")
*Childhood Years—A Memoir* (*Yōshō jidai*)
"Chronique inhumaine" ("Zangyakuki")
*Chvála stínů* (*In'ei raisan*)
*Dagboek van een oude dwaas* (*Fūten rōjin nikki*)
"Das Opfer" ("Shisei")
"De Dief" ("Watakushi")
"De la paresse" ("Randa no setsu")
*De sleutel* (*Kagi*)
*Deník bláznivého starce* (*Fūten rōjin nikki*)
"Der Dieb" ("Watakushi")
*Der Schlüssel* (*Kagi*)
*Diario di un vecchio pazzo* (*Fūten rōjin nikki*)
*Diary of a Mad Old Man* (*Fūten rōjin nikki*)
*Die Erzählung eines Blinden* (*Mōmoku monogatari*)
*Die geheime Geschichte des Fürsten von Musashi* (*Bushūkō hiwa*)
*Die Schwestern Makioka* (*Sasameyuki*)
"Die Tätowierung" ("Shisei")
"Die Traumbrücke" ("Yume no ukihashi")
"Divagazioni sull'otium" ("Randa no setsu")
*Dziennik szalonego starca* (*Fūten rōjin nikki*)
*Egy hibbant vénember naplója* (*Fūten rōjin nikki*)
"Ein kleines Königreich" ("Chiisana ōkoku")
*Eine Katze, ein Mann und zwei Frauen* (*Neko to Shōzō to futari no onna*)
*El la vivo de Syunkin* (*Shunkinshō*)
"El ladrón" ("Watakushi")
"El puente de los sueños" ("Yume no ukihashi")
"El tatuado" ("Shisei")
*Éloge de l'ombre* (*In'ei raisan*)
*Elogio de las sombras* (*In'ei raisan*)
*Enredadera de Yoshino* (*Yoshino kuzu*)
*Fino ad essere abbandonato* (*Suterareru made*)
*Gli insetti preferiscono le ortiche* (*Tade kuu mushi*)
"Hassan Khan le magicien" ("Hassan Kan no yōjutsu")
*Hay quien prefiere las ortigas* (*Tade kuu mushi*)
*Het geheim van de heer van Musashi* (*Bushūkō hiwa*)
"Histoire de A et B" ("A to B no hanashi")
*Histoire de Tomoda et Matsunaga* (*Tomoda to Matsunaga no hanashi*)
*Histoire secrète du sire de Musashi* (*Bushūkō hiwa*)
"I canneti" ("Ashikari")
"I due novizi" ("Futari no chigo")
"I piedi di Fumiko" ("Fumiko no ashi")
"Ich" ("Watakushi")
"Il censore" ("Ken'etsukan")
"Il demone" (Prima parte) ("Akuma")
"Il demone" (Seconda parte) ("Zoku akuma")
"Il dramma stregato" ("Norowareta gikyoku")

# 6

# Writings on Tanizaki

The * marks works that I have not seen, but that are mentioned in other lists.

Aira, César. "Sobre una novela de Tanizaki" [*Manji*]. *Tokonoma* 2 (Spring 1994): 63-68.

Alston, Patrick L. "The Learning Heart: Western and Native Education in Ivan Turgenev's *Nest of Gentry* and Tanizaki Jun'ichiro's *Light Snow* (*Makioka Sisters*)." *Acta Slavica Iaponica* 9 (1991): 108-15.

Anderer, Paul. Review of Tanizaki Jun'ichirō, *Childhood Years: A Memoir* [*Yōshō jidai*], trans. Paul McCarthy. *Monumenta Nipponica* 43.4 (1988): 473-75.

Arland, Marcel. "*Puisque je l'aime*, par Tanizaki." *La Nouvelle Revue Française* 26 (1926): 242-43.

Bardsley, Jan. Review of *Visions of Desire: Tanizaki's Fictional Worlds*, by Ken K. Ito. *Journal of the Association of Teachers of Japanese* 26.1 (April 1992): 74-77.

Bayard-Sakai, Anne. "L'irradiation de l'ombre." *La Recherche photographique* (December 1991): 49-51.

____________. "Le texte contre la littérature, autour du *Traité d'écriture* (*Bunshô tokuhon*) de Tanizaki Jun.ichirô." In *Littératures d'Extrême-Orient au XXe siècle*: *Essais*, 164-74. Arles: Editions Philippe Picquier, 1993.

____________. "Notice." In Tanizaki, *Œuvres* 1: "Terreur" ("Kyōfu," 1630-31); "La haine" ("Zōnen," 1634-35); "Le pied de Fumiko" ("Fumiko no ashi," 1721-25); *Un amour insensé* (*Chijin no ai*, 1747-51); *Histoire de Tomoda et Matsunaga* (*Tomoda to Matsunaga no hanashi*, 1768-70); "La mèche" ("Hitofusa no kami," 1776-77). Paris: Gallimard, 1997.

____________. "Notice." In Tanizaki, *Œuvres* 2: *Bruine de neige* (*Sasameyuki*, 1391-95); *La clef* (*Kagi*, 1508-14). Paris: Gallimard, 1998.

____________. "The Double Face of Writing." In *A Tanizaki Feast: The International Symposium in Venice*, ed. Adriana Boscaro and Anthony H. Chambers, 93-99. Michigan Monograph Series in Japanese Studies 24. Ann Arbor: Center for Japanese Studies, The University of Michigan, 1998.

Beonio-Brocchieri, Paolo. "La casa di Tanizaki." In *Dino Formaggio e l'estetica*, ed. Dino Formaggio et al., 103-7. Milano: UNICOPLI, 1985.

Bernardi, Joanne R. "The Early Development of the *Gendaigeki* Screenplay: Kaeriyama Norimasa, Kurihara Tōmas, Tanizaki Jun'ichirō and the Pure Film Movement." Ph.D. diss., Columbia University, 1992.

____________. "Tanizaki Jun'ichirō's 'The Present and Future of the Moving Pictures'." In *Currents in Japanese Cultures: Translations and Transformations*, ed. Amy Vladeck Heinrich, 291-308. New York: Columbia University Press, 1997.

____________. "The Literary Link: Tanizaki and the Pure Film Movement." In *A Tanizaki Feast: The International Symposium in Venice*, ed. Adriana Boscaro and Anthony H. Chambers, 75-92. Michigan Monograph Series in Japanese Studies 24. Ann Arbor: Center for Japanese Studies, The University of Michigan, 1998.

Berry, Margaret. "Meredith and Tanizaki on Modern Love." *Asian Profile* 11.3 (June 1983): 309-16.

Bienati, Luisa. "Innocenti perversioni: *Shōnen* di Tanizaki Jun'ichirō." *Il Giappone* 25 ([1985] 1987): 105-13.

____________. "Bellezza e crudeltà: la ristampa di *Neve sottile* e l'opera di Tanizaki." *Linea d'ombra* 8.49 (1990): 23-27.

____________. "Sacro e profano." In Tanizaki Jun'ichirō, *I piedi di Fumiko—Ave Maria*, 145-51. Venezia: Marsilio, 1995.

____________. "Un paradiso di morte." In Tanizaki Jun'ichirō, *La morte d'oro*, 11-38. Venezia: Marsilio, 1996.

____________. "La vita, le opere." In Tanizaki Jun'ichirō, *La morte d'oro*, 39-56. Venezia: Marsilio, 1996. Revised version in Tanizaki Jun'ichirō, *Yoshino*, ed. Adriana Boscaro, 37-53. Venezia: Marsilio, 1998.

Boscaro, Adriana. "Notizia biobibliografica." In Tanizaki Jun'ichirō, *L'amore di uno sciocco*, xv-xx. Milano: Bompiani, 1981.

____________. "Postfazione." In Tanizaki Jun'ichirō, *Pianto di sirena*, 113-20. Milano: Feltrinelli, 1985.

____________. "Il grande vecchio" (vii-xxxiv), "Cronologia" (xxxv-xlviii), "La fortuna di Tanizaki in Italia" (1155-68). In Tanizaki, *Opere*. Milano: Bompiani, 1988.

____________. "The Enchantment of a Myth: Tanizaki's Fictional West." *The Japan Foundation Newsletter* 20.2 (October 1992): 1-6. Spanish translation by Amalia Sato, "La Fascinación de un mito: el Occidente novelesco de Tanizaki." *Tokonoma* 1 (Summer 1994): 37-47.

____________. "Nota." In Tanizaki Jun'ichirō, *Storia di Tomoda e Matsunaga*, 109-14. Venezia: Marsilio, 1994.

____________. "Un omaggio al Grande Vecchio (1886-1965)." In Tanizaki Jun'ichirō, *Divagazioni sull'otium e altri scritti*, ed. Adriana Boscaro, 9-18. Venezia: Cafoscarina, 1995.

____________. "Introduzione." In Tanizaki Jun'ichirō, *Vita segreta del signore di Bushū*, v-xiii. Milano: Bompiani, 1996.

____________. "Il fascino dell'illusione: sogno e realtà nell'opera di Tanizaki Jun'ichirō." In *Immagini da sogno e frammenti della realtà—Il Giappone moderno tra cinema e letteratura*, ed. Nicoletta Spadavecchia and Muramatsu Mariko, 26-29. Milano: Consolato Generale del Giappone et al., 1996.

____________. "Tanizaki a Venezia, 5-8 aprile 1995." *Asiatica Venetiana* 1 (1996): 225-28.

_____________. "Il 'sapore della Cina' in Tanizaki." In *Studi in onore di Lionello Lanciotti*, ed. Sandra Marina Carletti, Maurizia Sacchetti, and Paolo Santangelo, 133-43. Napoli: Istituto Universitario Orientale, 1996.

_____________. "Lo specchio della memoria." In Tanizaki Jun'ichirō, *Yoshino*, 11-35. Venezia: Marsilio, 1998.

_____________ and Anthony Hood Chambers, eds. *A Tanizaki Feast: The International Symposium in Venice*. Michigan Monograph Series in Japanese Studies 24. Ann Arbor: Center for Japanese Studies, The University of Michigan, 1998. For the contents see under: Orsi, Maria Teresa; McCarthy, Paul; Ito, K. Ken; Liman, A.V.; Suzuki Sadami; Keene, Donald; Tschudin, Jean-Jacques; Bernardi, Joanne R.; Bayard-Sakai, Anne; Hijiya-Kirschnereit, Irmela; Pigeot, Jacqueline; Kōno Taeko; Chiba Shunji; Chambers, Anthony H.; Johnston, William; Boscaro, Adriana; Hibbett, Howard; Richie, Donald.
Preface: vii-xi; Chronology of Tanizaki Jun'ichirō: 171-74; Contributors: 175-77.

_____________. "In Pursuit of the Prints of Those Feet." In *A Tanizaki Feast: The International Symposium in Venice*, ed. Adriana Boscaro and Anthony H. Chambers, 151-55. Michigan Monograph Series in Japanese Studies 24. Ann Arbor: Center for Japanese Studies, The University of Michigan, 1998.

_____________. "Il gioco degli inganni. Tanizaki: la realtà e la fantasia." *Romanian Journal of Japanese Studies* 1 (1999): 3-13.

Calza, Gian Carlo. "Postfazione." In Tanizaki Jun'ichirō, *Libro d'ombra*, 91-111. Milano: Bompiani, 1982.

Cecchi, Annie. "Perspectives Multiples, Voyeurisme et Mise en Abyme: *Yabu no naka* [Dans le fourré] d'Akutagawa Ryûnosuke, *Les Faux-Monnayeurs* d'André Gide, *Kagi* [La Confession impudique] de Tanizaki Jun.ichirô." In *Japon pluriel: Actes du premier colloque de la Société française des études japonaises*, ed. Patrick Beillevaire and Anne Gossot, 437-43. Arles: Philippe Picquier, 1995.

Chambers, Anthony H. "Tanizaki Junichirō's Historical Fiction." *Journal of the Association of Teachers of Japanese* 8.1 (1972): 35-43.

_____________. "Tradition in the works of Tanizaki Jun'ichirō." Ph.D. diss., The University of Michigan, 1974.

_____________. "Tradition and Innovation in Tanizaki's *Ashikari*." In *Studia Asiatica*, ed. Laurence G. Thompson, 381-97. San Francisco: Chinese Material Center, 1975.

_____________. "A Study of Tanizaki's *Shōshō Shigemoto no haha*." *Harvard Journal of Asiatic Studies* 38.2 (1978): 357-79.

_____________. "Postscript to 'A Portrait of Shunkin'—*Shunkinshō Kōgo* by Tanizaki Jun'ichirō." *Monumenta Nipponica* 35.4 (1980): 457-60.

_____________. "A Study of Tanizaki's *Yoshino kuzu*." *Harvard Journal of Asiatic Studies* 41.2 (1981): 483-505.

_____________. "Introduction." In Tanizaki Jun'ichirō, *The Secret History of the Lord of Musashi and Arrowroot*, vii-xii. New York: Alfred A. Knopf, 1982.

_____________. "Introduction." In Tanizaki Jun'ichirō, *Naomi*, v-x. New York: Alfred A. Knopf, 1985.

———. "Recognizing and Translating Covert Irony in Japanese Literature." In *Rethinking Japan,* ed. Adriana Boscaro, Franco Gatti, and Massimo Raveri. Vol. 1, 116-20. Sandgate: Japan Library, 1991.

———. *The Secret Window: Ideal Worlds in Tanizaki's Fiction.* Harvard East Asian Monographs 167. Cambridge, Mass. and London: Harvard University Press, 1994.

———. "*The Makioka Sisters* as a Political Novel." In *A Tanizaki Feast: The International Symposium in Venice*, ed. Adriana Boscaro and Anthony H. Chambers, 133-38. Michigan Monograph Series in Japanese Studies 24. Ann Arbor: Center for Japanese Studies, The University of Michigan, 1998.

———. "Tanizaki Jun'ichirō." In *Encyclopedia of Literary Translation*. London: Fitzroy Dearborn, forthcoming.

Chiba, Shunji. "*The Makioka Sisters* as an *Emaki*." In *A Tanizaki Feast: The International Symposium in Venice*, ed. Adriana Boscaro and Anthony H. Chambers, 125-31. Michigan Monograph Series in Japanese Studies 24. Ann Arbor: Center for Japanese Studies, The University of Michigan, 1998.

Ciccarella, Emanuele. "Postfazione." In Tanizaki Jun'ichirō, *Il veleno di Afrodite*, 180-96. Milano: Garzanti, 1994.

———. "L'estetica empirica di Tanizaki Jun'ichirō." *Il Giappone* 32 ([1992] 1994): 129-44.

Ciferri, Ludovico. "Tanizaki, manie di bellezza. A trent'anni dalla morte l'editoria italiana riscopre lo scrittore giapponese." *Leggere* 71 (June 1995): 49-50.

Dale, Peter N. "The Linguistics of Silence" [on Tanizaki's *Bunshō tokuhon*]. Chap. 6 in *The Myth of Japanese Uniqueness,* 77-99. London: Routledge, 1988.

Daly, Saralyn R. "Tanizaki's West: a Fable of the Occident." In *Discovering the Other: Humanities East and West*, ed. Robert S. Ellwood, 103-21. Malinu: Undena Publications, 1984.

De Vos, Patrick. "Notice." In Tanizaki, *Œuvres* 1: "Histoire de A et B" ("A to B no hanashi," 1730-33). Paris: Gallimard, 1997.

de Vroomen, Pim. "Nawoord." In Junichiro Tanizaki, *Lof der schaduw.* Amsterdam: Meulenhoff, 1994.

DeZure, Deborah. "Tanizaki's 'The Bridge of Dreams' from the Perspective of *Amae* Psychology." *Literature and Psychology* 35.1 & 2 (1989): 46-65.

Epistola, Silvino V. "One Who Preferred Nettles (A Note on Tanizaki as Novelist)." *Asian Studies* 11.1 (1973): 1-27.

Falke, Wayne. "Tanizaki: Opponent of Naturalism." *Critique* 8.3 (Spring-Summer 1966): 19-25.

Fernandez, Jaime. "A Study of Tanizaki's *The Key.*" In *Approaches to the Modern Japanese Novel*, ed. Kinya Tsuruta and Thomas E. Swann, 215-29. Tokyo: Sophia, 1976.

Fogel, Joshua A. "Japanese Literary Travelers in Prewar China" [on Tanizaki's visits to China]. *Harvard Journal of Asiatic Studies* 49.2 (1989): 575-602.

Fontanille, Jacques. "Le Ralentissement et le rêve: À propos de *L'Eloge de l'ombre* de Tanizaki." Chap. 5 in *Sémiotique du Visible: Des mondes de lumière*, 159-92. Paris, Presses Universitaires de France, 1995. [A shorter version of a previous article published in *Nouveaux Actes Semiotiques* 26-27 (1993).]

Fowler, Edward. "Tanizaki's Sentimental Education" [Afterword to *Longing for Mother*]. *Monumenta Nipponica* 35.4 (1980): 479-83.

Fujii, James A. Review of *Visions of Desire: Tanizaki's Fictional Worlds*, by Ken K. Ito. *Modern Language Quarterly* 55.1 (1994): 114-19.

*Furukawa, Hiroyuki. "Tanizaki says, 'I am Not a Great Admirer of Oscar Wilde': A Note on Tanizaki's Translation of *Lady Windermere's Fan*." *Gaikoku bungaku kenkyū kiyō* 1 (1973): 1-27.

Gangloff, Eric J. "Tanizaki's Use of Traditional Literature: A Comparison of *Manji* and *Shinjū Ten no Amijima*." *Journal of the Association of Teachers of Japanese* 11.2 & 3 (1976): 217-34.

Geddes, Ward. "Dialect in Tanizaki's *Shunkinshō*." *Monumenta Nipponica* 39.4 (1984): 435-43.

Gerow, Aaron. "Celluloid Masks: The Cinematic Image and the Image of Japan." *Iris* 16 (Spring 1993): 23-36.

Gessel, Van C. "An Infatuation with Modernity: Tanizaki Jun'ichirō." In *Three Modern Novelists: Sōseki, Tanizaki, Kawabata,* 68-132. Tokyo: Kodansha International, 1993.

Ginzburg, Natalia. "Prefazione." In Tanizaki Jun'ichirō, *Gli insetti preferiscono le ortiche*, ix-xv. Milano: Mondadori, 1984.

Golley, Gregory L. "Tanizaki Jun'ichirō: The Art of Subversion and the Subversion of Art." *The Journal of Japanese Studies* 21.2 (1995): 365-404.

Goody, Ila. "The Stone Goddess and the Frozen Mother: Accomplices of Desire and Death in Tanizaki, *Tay John*, and *Obasan*." In *Nature and Identity in Canadian and Japanese Literature*, ed. Kinya Tsuruta and Theodore Goossen, 143-66. Toronto: University of Toronto-York University Joint Centre for Asia Pacific Studies, 1988.

Gunn, Giles B. "Tradition and Modernity in Modern Japanese Fiction: Variations on a Theme in Natsume Sōseki, Tanizaki Junichirō and Dazai Osamu." *Japan Christian Quarterly* 25 (Spring 1969): 96-106.

Hanson, Larry. "The Divided Self in Tanizaki and Stevenson." *Poetica* 44 (1995): 65-83.

Harper, Thomas J. "Afterword." In Tanizaki Jun'ichirō, *In Praise of Shadows*, 43-48. New Haven, Conn.: Leete's Island Book, 1977.

Hibbett, Howard. "Tanizaki and the Fatal Woman." In *Tanizaki Jun'ichirō kenkyū*, ed. Ara Masahito, 652-61. Tokyo: Yagi Shoten, 1972.

______________. "Fantasy in the Fiction of Tanizaki Junichiro." In *Studies on Japanese Culture*, ed. Ōta Saburō and Fukuda Rikutarō. Vol. 1, 252-56. Tokyo: Japan P.E.N. Club, 1973. Also in Italian translation, "La fantasia nella narrativa di Tanizaki Junichiro," as "Introduzione" in Tanizaki Jun'ichirō, *Neve sottile*, 11-17. Milano: Longanesi, 1973.

______________. "Comic Mischief." In *A Tanizaki Feast: The International Symposium in Venice*, ed. Adriana Boscaro and Anthony H. Chambers, 157-62. Michigan Monograph Series in Japanese Studies 24. Ann Arbor: Center for Japanese Studies, The University of Michigan, 1998.

Hijiya-Kirschnereit, Irmela. "Nachwort." In Tanizaki Jun'ichirō, *Die geheime Geschichte des Fürsten von Musashi*, 201-12. Frankfurt: Insel Verlag, 1994.

______________. Review of *The Secret Window: Ideal Worlds in Tanizaki's Fiction,* by Anthony H. Chambers. *The Journal of Asian Studies* 54.4 (1995): 1094-96.

______________. "Tanizaki's Art of Storytelling." In *A Tanizaki Feast: The International Symposium in Venice*, ed. Adriana Boscaro and Anthony H. Chambers, 101-5. Michigan Monograph Series in Japanese Studies 24. Ann Arbor: Center for Japanese Studies, The University of Michigan, 1998.

Hirai, Masako. "*The Makioka Sisters* and the Sisters of Jane Austen and George Eliot." In *The Force of Vision: Proceedings of the XIIIth Congress of the International Comparative Literature Association/Actes du XIIIème Congrès de l'Association Internationale de Littérature Comparée*. Vol. 1, *Dramas of Desire 2*, ed. Ziva Ben-Porat and Hana Wirth-Nesher, 55-63. ICLA '91. Tokyo: International Comparative Literature Association, 1995.

Hoop, Matthias. *Doppelspiel der Narration: Text, Autor und Protagonist in der Erzählung* "Kozō no yume" *von Tanizaki Jun'ichirō*. Iaponia Insula, Studien zu Kultur und Gesellschaft Japans 2. Wiesbaden: Harrassowitz Verlag, 1994.

Hosillos, Lucilla. "Tanizaki's *The Makioka Sisters* as a Reflection of the Dialectics of the Modernization of Japan." In *Studies on Japanese Culture*, ed. Ōta Saburō and Fukuda Rikutarō. Vol. 1, 270-80. Tokyo: Japan P.E.N. Club, 1973.

Hyman, Stanley Edgar. "A Japanese Master." *The New Leader* 46.20 (30 September 1963): 14-15.

Inouye, Charles Shirō. "Flowers in a Mirror: The 'Purely Japanese' Izumi Kyōka" [Tanizaki on Kyōka]. *The Japan Foundation Newsletter* 22.2 (July 1994): 18-21.

Ireland, Kenneth R. "Epics of Decline: The Institution of the Family in Thomas Mann's *Buddenbrooks* and Junichirō Tanizaki's *The Makioka Sisters*." *Arcadia-Zeitschrift für Vergleichende Literaturwissenschaft* 18.1 (1983): 39-49.

Ito, Ken K. "Tanizaki's Vision of the 'West'." Ph.D. diss., Yale University, 1985.

____________. Review of Tanizaki Jun'ichirō, *Naomi* [*Chijin no ai*], trans. Anthony H. Chambers. *Monumenta Nipponica* 41.3 (1986): 356-58.

____________. Review of Tanizaki Jun'ichirō, *Childhood Years: A Memoir* [*Yōshō jidai*], trans. Paul McCarthy. *The Journal of Asian Studies* 48.1 (1989): 181-83.

____________.*Visions of Desire: Tanizaki's Fictional Worlds*. Stanford: Stanford University Press, 1991.

____________."*Seven Japanese Tales* by Tanizaki Jun'ichirō." In *Masterworks of Asian Literature in Comparative Perspective: A Guide for Teaching*, ed. Barbara Stoler Miller, 428-38. Armonk, N.Y., London: M. E. Sharpe, 1994.

____________. "Tanizaki Jun'ichirō." In *Dictionary of Literary Biography*. Vol. 180, *Japanese Fiction Writers, 1868-1945*, ed. Van C. Gessel, 216-31. Detroit, Washington, D.C., London: A Bruccoli Clark Layman Book, Gale Research, 1997.

____________. "Prefacing 'Sorrows of a Heretic'." In *A Tanizaki Feast: The International Symposium in Venice*, ed. Adriana Boscaro and Anthony H. Chambers, 21-32. Michigan Monograph Series in Japanese Studies 24. Ann Arbor: Center for Japanese Studies, The University of Michigan, 1998.

Jeon, Miseli. "The Theme of *Hahakoi* in *The Makioka Sisters* (Sasameyuki)." In *Mothers in Japanese Literature*, ed. Kinya Tsuruta, 185-206. Vancouver: The University of British Columbia, Department of Asian Studies, 1997.

Johnston, William. "Illness, Disease, and Medicine in Three Novels by Tanizaki." In *A Tanizaki Feast: The International Symposium in Venice*, ed. Adriana Boscaro and Anthony H. Chambers, 139-50. Michigan Monograph Series in Japanese Studies 24. Ann Arbor: Center for Japanese Studies, The University of Michigan, 1998.

Jones, Sumie. "How Tanizaki Disarms the Intellectual Reader." *Literature East & West* 18.2-4 (1978): 321-29.

Kamei, Shunsuke. "Tanizaki Jun'ichirō's Modernism and His Relish for China." *Tamkang Review: A Quarterly of Comparative Studies Between Chinese and Foreign Literatures* 18.1-4 (Autumn 1987-Summer 1988): 199-206.

Karatani, Kōjin. "On the Power to Construct, Part II: The 'Novel without Plot' Debate." Chap. 6 in *Origins of Modern Japanese Literature,* ed. Brett de Bary, 155-72. Durham, N.C. and London: Duke University Press, 1993.

Keene, Donald. "Tanizaki Junichirō." Chap. 4 in *Landscapes and Portraits: Appreciations of Japanese Culture,* 171-85. Tokyo and Palo Alto: Kodansha International, 1971. Reprinted in *Appreciations of Japanese Culture*, 171-85. Tokyo and Palo Alto: Kodansha International, 1981.

_____________. "Tanizaki Junichirō." Chap. 20 in *Dawn to the West: Japanese Culture of the Modern Era: Fiction*, 720-85. New York: Holt, Rinehart and Winston, 1984.

_____________. "The Plays of Tanizaki." In *A Tanizaki Feast: The International Symposium in Venice*, ed. Adriana Boscaro and Anthony H. Chambers, 55-64. Michigan Monograph Series in Japanese Studies 24. Ann Arbor: Center for Japanese Studies, The University of Michigan, 1998.

Kimball, Arthur G. "The Last Extremity." Chap. 6 in *Crisis in Identity and Contemporary Japanese Novels*, 109-14. Tokyo: Tuttle, 1973.

Kōno, Taeko. "Presentiments." In *A Tanizaki Feast: The International Symposium in Venice*, ed. Adriana Boscaro and Anthony H. Chambers, 117-24. Michigan Monograph Series in Japanese Studies 24. Ann Arbor: Center for Japanese Studies, The University of Michigan, 1998.

Kristeva, Tzvetana. "Vazhvala na syankata." In Tanizaki Jun'ichirō, *Portret na Shunkin*, 5-12. Sofia: Narodna Kultura, 1982.

Lamarre, Thomas. "The deformation of the modern spectator: synaesthesia, cinema, and the spectre of race in Tanizaki." *Japan Forum* 11.1 (1999): 23-42.

Lewell, John. "Tanizaki Jun'ichirō." Entry in *Modern Japanese Novelists: A Biographical Dictionary,* 399-421. Tokyo: Kodansha International, 1993.

Liman, Anthony V. "The True Mark of the Saint: Robertson Davies' *Fifth Business* and Jun'ichirō Tanizaki's *A Portrait of Shunkin*." In *Nature and Identity in Canadian and Japanese Literature,* ed. Kinya Tsuruta and Theodore Goossen, 87-108. Toronto: University of Toronto/York University Joint Centre for Asia Pacific Studies, 1988.

_____________. "The White Mother of All Things in *Yoshino kuzu*." In *Mothers in Japanese Literature,* ed. Kinya Tsuruta, 159-84. Vancouver: The University of British Columbia, Department of Asian Studies, 1997.

_____________. "Scripting the Role: Woman as Stage Text in Tanizaki's *Diary of a Mad Old Man*." *Asiatica Venetiana* 2 (1997): 93-103.

_____________. "The Maternal Landscape of 'Longing for Mother'." In *A Tanizaki Feast: The International Symposium in Venice*, ed. Adriana Boscaro and Anthony H. Chambers, 33-40. Michigan Monograph Series in Japanese Studies 24. Ann Arbor: Center for Japanese Studies, The University of Michigan, 1998.

Lippit, Noriko M. "The Plot Controversy Between Tanizaki and Akutagawa." Chap. 3 in *Reality and Fiction in Modern Japanese Literature*, 55-69. "Western Dark Romanticism and Japan's Aesthetic Literature." Chap. 4 in ibid., 70-81. "Tanizaki and Poe: the Grotesque and the Quest for Supernal Beauty." Chap. 5 in ibid., 82-103. London: The Macmillan Press, 1980. Chap. 5 first published in *Comparative Literature* 29.3 (Summer 1977): 221-40.

*Long, Margherita. "Skirmishes with Sexual 'Difference': Tanizaki's Experiments in Masochism, 1931-1933." Ph.D. diss., Princeton University, 1998.

Lyons, Phyllis I. "The Years of Living Dangerously: Life and Love in Tanizaki's Fiction of 1928-30." In *Love and Sexuality in Japanese Literature,* ed. Eiji Sekine. Proceedings of the Midwest Association for Japanese Literary Studies (PMAJLS), vol. 5 (Summer 1999), forthcoming.

Malatesta, Hiroko Morita. "The Way of Modern Japanese Fiction: The Concept of 'Geidō' and the Novels of Tanizaki Jun'ichirō and Kawabata Yasunari." Ph.D. diss., University of California, Los Angeles, 1980.

Marks, Alfred H. "After Tanizaki, Mishima and Kawabata, What?" In *Studies on Japanese Culture*, ed. Ōta Saburō and Fukuda Rikutarō. Vol. 1, 326-30. Tokyo: Japan P.E.N. Club, 1973.

Matsui, Sakuko. "View of an Elder Novelist. A Consideration of Tanizaki Jun'ichirō on Sōseki's 'Meian'." *Journal of the Oriental Society of Australia* 15-16 (1983-84): 126-36.

McCarthy, Paul F. "The Early Life and Works of Tanizaki Jun'ichirō." Ph.D. diss., Harvard University, 1975.

____________. "The Madonna and the Harlot: Images of Woman in Tanizaki." *Japanese Journal of Religious Studies* 9.2-3 (1982): 235-55.

____________. Review of Junichirō Tanizaki, *The Secret History of the Lord of Musashi and Arrowroot* [*Bushūkō hiwa* and *Yoshino kuzu*], trans. Anthony H. Chambers. *Monumenta Nipponica* 38.3 (1983): 321-23.

____________. "Tanizaki's Literary Exoticism: A Case of Probable Western Influence." *Ei-Bei bungaku* (Rikkyō daigaku) 44 (1984): 109-24.

____________. "The Traditional and the Modern in Three Works of Tanizaki Jun'ichirō." *Rikkyō Daigaku kenkyū hōkoku 'Jinbun kagaku'* 43 (1984): 17-38.

____________. "Images of Woman as Mother in Tanizaki's Fiction." *The Transactions of the Asiatic Society of Japan* 4th ser., 1 (1986): 23-44.

____________. "Tanizaki Jun'ichirō's 'Infantile Eroticism'." *Surugadai University Studies* 2 (1988): 17-29.

____________. "Introduction." In Tanizaki Jun'ichiro, *Childhood Years: A Memoir*, v-xiii. Tokyo: Kodansha International, 1988.

____________. "Preface." In Tanizaki Jun'ichiro, *A Cat, a Man, and Two Women*, vii-xiv. Tokyo: Kodansha International, 1990.

____________. "Beauty and Illusion: Tanizaki in Venice." *Monumenta Nipponica* 50.4 (1995): 523-28.

____________. "Nabokov's *Lolita* and Tanizaki's *Naomi*: a Comparative Essay." *Surugadai University Studies* 12 (1996): 163-76.

____________. "The West as Other." In *A Tanizaki Feast: The International Symposium in Venice*, ed. Adriana Boscaro and Anthony H. Chambers, 15-20. Michigan Monograph Series in Japanese Studies 24. Ann Arbor: Center for Japanese Studies, The University of Michigan, 1998.

McClellan, Edwin. Review of Tanizaki Jun'ichirō, *The Key*, trans. Howard Hibbett. *Monumenta Nipponica* 16.1-2 (1960): 205-11.

McDonald, Keiko I. "Rhetorical Stance in Tanizaki's *The Key*." *The Japan Interpreter* 11.2 (1976): 203-12.

____________. "A Reassessment of *Some Prefer Nettles*." *Journal of the Association of Teachers of Japanese* 12.2-3 (1977): 195-210.

Mécréant, Mark. "Notice." In Tanizaki, *Œuvres* 1: "Le secret" ("Himitsu," 1626-27); "Morosités d'un hérétique" ("Itansha no kanashimi," 1696-99); "Affres d'un jeune garçon" ("Aru shōnen no osore," 1726-28). Paris: Gallimard, 1997.

Melanowicz, Mikołaj. "Native Tradition in the Literature of Tanizaki Jun'ichirō." In *Studies on Japanese Culture*, ed. Ōta Saburō and Fukuda Rikutarō. Vol. 1, 346-50. Tokyo: Japan P.E.N. Club, 1973.

______________. *Tanizaki Jun'ichirō a krąg japońskiej tradycji rodzimej*. Warszawa: Wydawnictwa Uniwersytetu Warszawskiego, 1976.

______________. "Narrator and Character in Japanese Prose: A Discussion Based on Tanizaki Jun'ichirō's Work." *Zagadnienia rodzajów literackich* 19.2 (1976): 63-83.

______________. "Time in the Novels of Tanizaki Jun'ichirō." In *European Studies on Japan*, ed. Ian Nish and Charles Dunn, 302-6. Tenterden: Paul Norbury, 1979.

______________. "Tradition in the Popular Novel *Rangiku Monogatari*." In *Tradition and Modern Japan*, ed. Patrick G. O'Neill, 217-23. Tenterden: Paul Norbury, 1981.

______________. "Ethos in the Novels by Jun'ichiro Tanizaki and Henryk Sienkiewicz." In *Japanese Civilization in the Modern World V: Culturedness*, ed. Tadao Umesao, Catherine C. Lewis, and Yasuyuki Kurita, 31-47. Senri Ethnological Studies 28. Osaka: National Museum of Ethnology, 1990.

______________. *Tanizaki: Japoński most snów.* Warszawa: Wydawnictwo Wilga, 1994.

Merken, Kathleen. "The Figure of the Old Man in the Fiction of Tanizaki." In *Life, Death and Age in Modern Japanese Fiction*, ed. Reiko Tsukimura, 13-20. Toronto: University of Toronto-York University, Joint Centre on Modern East Asia, 1978.

*______________."The Evolution of Tanizaki Jun'ichirō as a Narrative Artist." Ph.D. diss., The University of British Columbia, 1979.

______________. "Tanizaki Jun'ichirō: 'Tattoo,' 'The Tale of Shunkin,' 'The Bridge of Dreams.'" In *Approaches to the Modern Japanese Short Story,* ed. Kin'ya Tsuruta and Thomas Swann, 319-38. Tokyo: Waseda University Press, 1982.

Migeot, François. "L'ombre d'un doute, une lecture d'*Éloge de l'ombre*." In *Mélanges offerts à Jean Peytard* 1, 223-37. Annales Littéraires de l'Université de Besançon 502. Paris: Diffusion Les Belles Lettres, 1993.

Miller, Henry. "Préface." In Junichiro Tanizaki, *Deux amours cruelles*, 7-10. Paris: Stock, 1960.

Miura, Tokuhiro. "Tanizaki and the Tradition." In *Tanizaki Jun'ichirō kenkyū*, ed. Ara Masahito, 631-51. Tokyo: Yagi Shoten, 1972.

Miyoshi, Masao. "The Lure of the 'West': Tanizaki Junichirō." Chap. 5 in *Off Center: Power and Culture Relations between Japan and the United States*, 126-48. Cambridge, Mass.: Harvard University Press, 1991.

Montupet, Pascale. "The Palimpsest of Memory in *Yoshino-Kuzu* of Tanizaki Junichirō." In *Contemporary European Writing on Japan*, ed. Ian Nish, 241-44. Woodchurch Ashford Kent: Paul Norbury Publications, 1988.

______________. "Nouvelle et récit poétique: Coïncidences de *Sylvie* et *Yoshino-Kuzu*." In *The Force of Vision: Proceedings of the XIIIth Congress of the International Comparative Literature Association / Actes du XIIIème Congrès de l'Association Internationale de Littérature Comparée*. Vol. 3,

*Powers of Narration*, ed. Gerald Gillespie and André Lorant, 91-99. ICLA '91. Tokyo: International Comparative Literature Association, 1995.

Moravia, Alberto. "Prefazione." In Tanizaki Junichiro, *L'amore di uno sciocco*, vi-xi. Milano: Bompiani, 1981.

Mottola, Cinzia. "Postfazione." In Tanizaki Jun'ichirō, *Morbose fantasie*, 92-94. Milano: SE, 1994.

Mulhern, Chieko Irie. Review of Tanizaki Jun'ichirō, *Naomi* [*Chijin no ai*], trans. Anthony H. Chambers. *Journal of Asian Studies* 45.4 (1986): 863-65.

*Nakao, Seijo. "Regendered Artistry: Tanizaki Junichiro and the Tradition of Decadence." Ph.D. diss., New York University, 1992.

Napier, Susan J. Review of *Visions of Desire: Tanizaki's Fictional Worlds,* by Ken K. Ito. *Bulletin of the School of Oriental and African Studies* 56.3 (1993): 624-25.

Napolitano, Gian Gaspare. "Una visita a Tanizaki." In Tanizaki Jun'ichirō, *La Chiave*, 5-12. Milano: Mondadori, 1971.

Newton, Michael C. "The Autobiography of Illusion: Tanizaki's *Amae*." *Transactions of the International Conference of Orientalists in Japan* 22 (1977): 44-52.

Ninomiya, Masayuki. "Junichirô Tanizaki: une dialectique du réel et de l'imaginaire." In *Japon*, ed. Tamba Akira and Gilbert Lascaul, 153-58. Paris: Editions Jean-Michel Place, 1990.

_____________. "Préface." In Tanizaki, *Œuvres* 1, xi-lii. Paris: Gallimard, 1997.

_____________. "Préface." In Tanizaki, *Œuvres* 2, ix-xxxiv. Paris: Gallimard, 1998.

_____________. "L'espace et le mode de vie à travers les trois œuvres de Tanizaki Juni'ichirô, publiées dans les années 1923 et 1924: AVE MARIA, NIKKAI (Amas de chair) et CHIJIN NO AI (Un amour insensé)." *Asiatischen Studien / Etudes Asiatiques* 53.2 (1999): 293-301.

Noguchi, Takehiko. "Time in the World of *Sasameyuki*," trans. Teruko Craig. *Journal of Japanese Studies* 3.1 (1977): 1-36.

Nornes, Markus. "Context and *The Makioka Sisters*." *East-West Film Journal* 5.2 (July 1991): 46-68.

Ochner, Nobuko Miyama. "History and Fiction: Portrayals of Confucius by Tanizaki Jun'ichirō and Nakajima Atsushi." In *Literary Relations East and West: Selected Essays*, ed. Jean Toyama and Nobuko Ochner, 68-79. Honolulu: University of Hawaii at Manoa and the East-West Center, College of Languages, Linguistics and Literature, 1990.

_____________. Review of *Visions of Desire: Tanizaki's Fictional Worlds,* by Ken K. Ito. *Monumenta Nipponica* 47.4 (1992): 532-35.

O'Leary, Joseph S. "Jun'ichiro Tanizaki Meets Thomas Hardy." Summary of his presentation at the May 1999 meeting of the Asiatic Society of Japan. *Asiatic Society of Japan Bulletin* 6 (June 1999): 2-4.

Olson, Lawrence. "*The Makioka Sisters*. A Japanese Family Novel: A Great Work of Fiction Recommended to Historians and Sociologists." *East Asia Series* (American Universities Field Staff) 11.5 (1964): 533-41.

Orsi, Maria Teresa. "The Colors of Shadows." In *A Tanizaki Feast: The International Symposium in Venice*, ed. Adriana Boscaro and Anthony H. Chambers, 1-13. Michigan Monograph Series in Japanese Studies 24. Ann Arbor: Center for Japanese Studies, The University of Michigan, 1998.

Pampaloni, Geno. "Prefazione." In Tanizaki Junichiro, *La Chiave*, 13-21. Milano: Mondadori, 1971.

Parise, Goffredo. "Il 'casto' Tanizaki maestro di erotismo." *Corriere della Sera*, 26 January 1983. Reprinted in Goffredo Parise, *Opere*, ed. Bruno Callegher and Mauro Portello. Vol. 2, 1517-21. Milano: Mondadori, 1989.

Pasolini, Pier Paolo. "Junichiro Tanizaki—*Neve sottile.*" In *Descrizioni di descrizioni*, 278-82. Torino: Einaudi, 1979.

Petersen, Gwenn B. "Tanizaki Jun'ichirō." Chap. 2 in *The Moon in the Water: Understanding Tanizaki, Kawabata and Mishima*, 44-120. Honolulu: University Press of Hawaii, 1979.

Pigeot, Jacqueline. "L'éloge de l'ombre de Tanizaki." *Critique* 285 (February 1971): 132-48.

____________. "La métropole marginale." *Autrement* (hors série n. 8, Des Villes Nommées: Tokyo) (September 1984): 166-68.

____________. "Notice." In Tanizaki, *Œuvres* 1: "Le Kilin" ("Kirin," 1606-10); "Les deux novices" ("Futari no chigo," 1703-6); "Nostalgie de ma mère" ("Haha o kouru ki," 1715-19); *Le goût des orties* (*Tade kuu mushi*, 1778-84); *Yoshino* (*Yoshino kuzu*, 1792-804); *Le récit de l'aveugle* (*Mōmoku monogatari*, 1818-24); *Histoire secrète du sire de Musashi* (*Bushūkō hiwa*, 1838-42); *Éloge de l'ombre* (*In'ei raisan*, 1886-91). Paris: Gallimard, 1997.

____________. "L'époque de Heian dans *Shôshô Shigemoto no haha* (*La mère du général Shigemoto*) de Tanizaki." In *Le Vase de béryl: Études sur le Japon et la Chine en hommage à Bernard Frank*, ed. Jacqueline Pigeot and Hartmut O. Rotermund, 223-32. Arles: Editions Philippe Picquier, 1997.

____________. "Notice." In Tanizaki, *Œuvres* 2: *La mère du général Shigemoto* (*Shōshō Shigemoto no haha*, 1424-33). Paris: Gallimard, 1998.

____________. "The Function of Source References in *Arrowroot*." In *A Tanizaki Feast: The International Symposium in Venice*, ed. Adriana Boscaro and Anthony H. Chambers, 107-15. Michigan Monograph Series in Japanese Studies 24. Ann Arbor: Center for Japanese Studies, The University of Michigan, 1998.

Pincus, Leslie. "Transgressing the Frames of Fiction." *Japan Quarterly* 37.4 (October-December 1990): 433-49.

Pollack, David. "The Deviant Self: Jun'ichirō Tanizaki's *Some Prefer Nettles*." Part I, chap. 3 in *Reading Against Culture: Ideology and Narrative in the Japanese Novel*, 67-87. Ithaca and London: Cornell University Press, 1992.

Powell, Irena. Review of *Visions of Desire: Tanizaki's Fictional Worlds*, by Ken K. Ito. *Journal of the Royal Asiatic Society* 3.1 (April 1993): 180-82.

Richie, Donald. "The Film Adaptations." In *A Tanizaki Feast: The International Symposium in Venice*, ed. Adriana Boscaro and Anthony H. Chambers, 163-70. Michigan Monograph Series in Japanese Studies 24. Ann Arbor: Center for Japanese Studies, The University of Michigan, 1998.

Rimer, Thomas J. "Tanizaki Junichirō: The Past as Homage—*A Portrait of Shunkin and The Bridge of Dreams*." Chap. 2 in *Modern Japanese Fiction and Its Tradition: An Introduction*, 22-37. Princeton: Princeton University Press, 1978.

Rossi Salvagnini, Anna Maria. "Uno scrittore contemporaneo giapponese: Junichirô Tanizaki." *Il Giappone* 5 (1965): 115-22.

Rowley, G. G. "Yosano Akiko's *Shin-shin'yaku Genji monogatari* in Comparative Perspective." *Research Papers in Japanese Studies* 1, ed. Mark Teeuwen, 1-21. Cardiff: Cardiff Centre for Japanese Studies, University of Wales, 1996.

Rubin, Jay. "Tanizaki in Taishō." Chap. 14 in *Injurious to Public Morals: Writers and the Meiji State*, 235-45. Seattle: University of Washington Press, 1984.

______________. Review of *Visions of Desire: Tanizaki's Fictional Worlds*, by Ken K. Ito. *Harvard Journal of Asiatic Studies* 53.1 (1994): 268-71.

Saeki, Junko. "Reconsidering Tanizaki Jun'ichirō's Love and Eroticism: 'Iro' Tradition and Modern 'Ren'ai' in Japanese Literary History." In *Love and Sexuality in Japanese Literature,* ed. Eiji Sekine. Proceedings of the Midwest Association for Japanese Literary Studies (PMAJLS), vol. 5 (Summer 1999), forthcoming.

Sakai, Cécile. "Notice." In Tanizaki, *Œuvres* 1: "Les jeunes garçons" ("Shōnen," 1619-20); "Une mort dorée" ("Konjiki no shi," 1636-38); "Visions d'un lit de douleur" ("Byōjoku no gensō," 1677-79); "Le petit royaume" ("Chiisana ōkoku," 1711-12); *Le chat, son maître et ses deux maîtresses* (*Neko to Shōzō to futari no onna*, 1896-97). Paris: Gallimard, 1997.

______________. "Notice." In Tanizaki, *Œuvres* 2: *Journal d'un vieux fou* (*Fūten rōjin nikki*, 1553-58). Paris: Gallimard, 1998.

Sakaki, Atsuko. "A Gallery of 'Severed Heads': A Comparative Study of Yumiko Kurahashi's *Popoi* [and Tanizaki's *Bushūkō hiwa*]." In *The Force of Vision: Proceedings of the XIIIth Congress of the International Comparative Literature Association / Actes du XIIIème Congrès de l'Association Internationale de Littérature Comparée.* Vol. 1, *Visions of Beauty*, ed. Roseann Runte and Hans R. Runte, 386-93. ICLA '91. Tokyo: International Comparative Literature Association, 1995.

______________."Japanese Perceptions of China: The Sinophilic Fiction of Tanizaki Jun'ichirō." *Harvard Journal of Asiatic Studies* 59.1 (1999): 187-218.

______________. "Doing Things with Words: Acts and Effects in Tanizaki Jun'ichirō's *Manji*." Chap. 5 in *Recontextualizing Texts: Narrative Performance in Modern Japanese Fiction*, 181-228. Harvard East Asian Monograph 180. Cambridge, Mass.: Harvard University Press, 1999.

Scott, Paul D. "Introduction." In "Japanese Travelogues of China in the 1920s: The Accounts of Akutagawa Ryūnosuke and Tanizaki Jun'ichirō." *Chinese Studies in History* (guest editor Joshua A. Fogel) 30.4 (Summer 1997): 56-70.

Seidensticker, Edward. "Introduction." In Tanizaki Junichiro, *Some Prefer Nettles*, vii-xvii. New York, Toronto: Alfred A. Knopf, 1955.

______________. "Kafū and Tanizaki." *Japan Quarterly* 12.4 (1965): 491-94.

______________. "Tanizaki Jun-ichirō, 1886-1965." *Monumenta Nipponica* 21.3-4 (1966): 249-65.

______________. "Introduction." In Tanizaki Junichirō, *The Makioka Sisters*, ix-xxiii. New York, Toronto: Alfred A. Knopf, 1993.

Sekine, Eiji. "Eroticism in the Absence of Sexuality: Tanizaki, Kawabata and Yoshiyuki." *Yearbook of Comparative and General Literature* (Bloomington, IN) (1993): 51-66.

______________. Review of *The Secret Window: Ideal Worlds in Tanizaki's Fiction*, by Anthony H. Chambers. *Journal of the Association of Teachers of Japanese* 30.1 (April 1996): 44-50.

Sherif, Ann. "'The Bridge of Dreams' and *Masks*: Two Modern Responses to the *Tale of Genji*." In *Approaches to Teaching Murasaki Shikibu's* "The Tale of Genji," ed. Edward Kamens, 148-54. New York: The Modern Languages Association of America, 1993.

Stalph, Jürgen. "Von Nasen und Zähren, ferner von Tanizaki Jun'ichirō und der Kunst seines Übersetzers Bohaczek, Verlangen nach mehr zu erzeugen." Review of Tanizaki Jun'ichirō, *Die geheime Geschichte des Fürsten von Musashi* [*Bushūkō hiwa*], trans. Josef Bohaczek. *Rundschreiben der Deutschen Gesellschaft für Völkerkunde Ostasiens* (January 1995): 6-9.

Starrs, Roy. Review of *The Secret Window: Ideal Worlds in Tanizaki's Fiction*, by Anthony H. Chambers. *Monumenta Nipponica* 50.3 (1995): 392-94.

Struve, Daniel. "Notice." In Tanizaki, *Œuvres* 1: *Le coupeur de roseaux* (*Ashikari*, 1851-59). Paris: Gallimard, 1997.

Suzuki, Sadami. "Tanizaki Jun'ichirō as Cultural Critic." *Japan Review* 7 (1996): 23-32.

_____________. "Eroticism, Grotesquerie, and Nonsense in Taishō Japan: Tanizaki's Response to Modern and Contemporary Culture." In *A Tanizaki Feast: The International Symposium in Venice*, ed. Adriana Boscaro and Anthony H. Chambers, 41-53. Michigan Monograph Series in Japanese Studies 24. Ann Arbor: Center for Japanese Studies, The University of Michigan, 1998.

Suzuki, Tomi. "Allegories of Modernity: Parodic Confession in Tanizaki Jun'ichirō *Fool's Love*." "Epilogue: Tanizaki's Speaking Subject and Creation of Tradition." Chap. 7 in *Narrating the Self: Fiction of Japanese Modernity*, 151-74; 175-86. Stanford: Stanford University Press, 1996.

Thonis, Luis. "Capullos caídos." In *Cuerpos Inéditos*, 61-86. Buenos Aires: Grupo Editor Latinoamericano, 1995.

Toyama, Jean. "To Other or Be Othered: de Beauvoir/Tanizaki, Where is *The Key*?" In *Significant Others: Gender and Culture in Film and Literature East and West*, ed. William Burgwinkle, Glenn Man, and Valerie Wayne, 105-12. Honolulu: College of Languages, Linguistics and Literature, University of Hawaii, 1993.

_____________. "Tanizaki's Naomi: Japanese Pygmalion Meets Westernized Vamp." In *Gender and Culture in Literature and Film East and West: Issues of Perception and Interpretation*, ed. Masavisut Nitaya, George Simson, and Larry E. Smith, 127-34. Honolulu: College of Languages, Linguistics and Literature, University of Hawaii, 1994.

_____________. "Triangulating the Voyeur or Desire and the Look." In *Love and Sexuality in Japanese Literature*, ed. Eiji Sekine. Proceedings of the Midwest Association for Japanese Literary Studies (PMAJLS). Vol. 5 (Summer 1999), forthcoming.

Tschudin, Jean-Jacques. "Notice." In Tanizaki, *Œuvres* 1: "Le tatouage" ("Shisei," 1595-601); *Le meurtre d'O-Tsuya* (*Otsuya koroshi*, 1647-51); "L'espion du Kaiser" ("Dokutan," 1664-69); "La complainte de la sirène" ("Ningyo no nageki," 1682-87); *O-Kuni et Gohei* (*Okuni to Gohei*, 1735-38); *La source au renard blanc* (*Byakko no yu*, 1742-45); *Mumyô et Aizen* (*Mumyō to Aizen*, 1756-59); "Le professeur Radô" — "Le professeur Radô revisité" ("Radō sensei" — "Zoku Radō sensei," 1762-64); *Shunkin, esquisse d'un portrait* (*Shunkinshō*, 1866-74); "Notice sur l'œuvre théâtrale" (1903-15). Paris: Gallimard, 1997.

_____________. "Du bon usage de l'énigme chez Tanizaki." In *Le Vase de béryl: Études sur le Japon et la Chine en hommage à Bernard Frank*, ed. Jacqueline Pigeot and Hartmut O. Rotermund, 233-41. Arles: Philippe Picquier, 1997.

_____________. “Tanizaki et le shi-shôsetsu ou du bon usage des matériaux autobiographiques.” In *Tours et détours: écritures autobiographiques dans les littératures chinoise et japonaise du XXe siècle,* ed. Chantal Andro, Annie Curien, and Cécile Sakai, 55-73. Paris: Publications universitaires Denis-Diderot, 1998.

_____________. “Notice.” In Tanizaki, *Œuvres* 2: *Années d'enfance* (*Yōshō jidai*, 1449-58); “Chronique inhumaine” (“Zangyakuki,” 1519-23); “Le pont flottant des songes” (“Yume no ukihashi,” 1527-35). Paris: Gallimard, 1998.

_____________. “Tanizaki and the *Shinkabuki*.” In *A Tanizaki Feast: The International Symposium in Venice*, ed. Adriana Boscaro and Anthony H. Chambers, 65-74. Michigan Monograph Series in Japanese Studies 24. Ann Arbor: Center for Japanese Studies, The University of Michigan, 1998.

Tsukimura, Reiko. “The Sense of Loss in *The Makioka Sisters*.” In *Approaches to the Modern Japanese Novel*, ed. Kinya Tsuruta and Thomas E. Swann, 230-40. Tokyo: Sophia, 1976.

Tsuruta, Kin'ya. “Images of Westerners in Tanizaki Jun'ichirō and Nakazato Tsuneko.” *The Japan Foundation Newsletter* 22.1 (1993): 11-20, 29.

Ueda, Makoto. “Tanizaki and His Idea of a Novel.” In *Studies on Japanese Culture*, ed. Ōta Saburō and Fukuda Rikutarō. Vol. 1, 451-60. Tokyo: Japan P.E.N. Club, 1973.

_____________. “Tanizaki Jun'ichirō.” Chap. 3 in *Modern Japanese Writers and the Nature of Literature*, 54-84. Stanford: Stanford University Press, 1976.

Vernon, Victoria V. “Creating Koharu: The Image of Woman in the Works of Kawabata Yasunari and Tanizaki Jun'ichirō.” Chap. 7 in *Daughters of the Moon: Wish, Will, and Social Constraint in Fiction by Modern Japanese Women*, 171-203. Berkeley: University of California, 1988.

Wilson, Michiko N. Review of *Visions of Desire: Tanizaki's Fictional Worlds*, by Ken K. Ito. *The Journal of Japanese Studies* 19.1 (1993): 261-67.

Wixted, John Timothy. “Dos Autores-Traductores Japoneses del Período Moderno: Mori Ōgai y Tanizaki Jun'ichiro,” trans. Ana Clelia Vincenti. In *Traducción como cultura*, ed. Lisa Bradford, 99-110. Rosario (Argentina): Beatriz Viterbo Editora, 1997.

Yamanouchi, Hisaaki. “The Eternal Womanhood: Tanizaki Jun'ichirō and Kawabata Yasunari.” Chap. 5 in *The Search for Authenticity in Modern Japanese Literature*, 107-36. Cambridge, London, New York: Cambridge University Press, 1978.

Yonogi, Reiko. “East and West in Tanizaki's Literature.” In *Facing East/Facing West: North America and the Asia/Pacific Region in the 1990s*, 393-99. Kalamazoo, Mich.: Western Michigan University, 1990.

# 7

# Index of Translators

Alegre, Edilberto N.
“Hōkan”

Anhava, Tuomas
*Kagi*

Anouilh, Paul
*Shōshō Shigemoto no haha*

Asada, S., H. Yokohama, and Charles Jacob
*Aisureba koso*

Barova, Dora
*Kagi*

Bayard-Sakai, Anne
“Hitofusa no kami,” *Kagi*, “Kyōfu,” “Randa no setsu,” *Tomoda to Matsunaga no hanashi*, “Zōnen”

Bell, Eric S., and Eiji Ukai
*Byakko no yu*, *Okuni to Gohei*

Benl, Oscar
*Chijin no ai*, *Fūten rōjin nikki*

Berndt, Jürgen, and Eiko Saito-Berndt
“Chiisana ōkoku”

Bienati, Luisa
“Ave Maria,” “Konjiki no shi,” “Shōnen”

Fredrisson, Nils
*Tade kuu mushi*

Gigli, Lorenzo
*Aisureba koso*

Göncz, Arpád
*Fūten rōjin nikki*

Groupe Kirin
"Kirin"

Harper, Thomas J., and Edward G. Seidensticker
*In'ei raisan*

Hibbett, Howard
"Aoi hana," *Fūten rōjin nikki*, *Kagi*, "Kyōfu," *Manji*, *Mōmoku monogatari*, "Shisei," *Shunkinshō*, "Watakushi," "Yume no ukihashi"

Hilská, Vlasta
*Otsuya koroshi*, *Tade kuu mushi*

Holti, Mária
"Shisei"

Hoop, Matthias
"Kozō no yume"

Humbert, Monique
"Shisei"

Humpherson, Roy, and Hajime Okita
*Ashikari*, *Shunkinshō*

Ijichi, Sumimasa
"Shisei"

Isiguro, Teruhiko
*Mumyō to Aizen*, *Okuni to Gohei*, "Shisei," *Shunkinshō* (with Masao Miyamoto)

Iwado, Zenchi
*Otsuya koroshi*

Kaila, Kai
"Aoi hana," "Kyōfu," *Mōmoku monogatari*, "Shisei," *Shunkinshō*, "Watakushi," "Yume no ukihashi"

Mécréant, Marc

"Aozukashi no hanashi," "Aru shōnen no osore," *Bushūkō hiwa*, *Chijin no ai*, "Hassan Kan no yōjutsu," "Himitsu," "Itansha no kanashimi," "Jinmenso," "Kin to gin," "Kyōto o omou," *Mumyō to Aizen*, "Norowareta gikyoku," *Sasameyuki*, "Shisei," "Tojō," "Yanagiyu no jiken," *Yōshō jidai*, "Zangyakuki"

Melanowicz, Mikołaj

*Ashikari*, *Fūten rōjin nikki*, *Shunkinshō*, *Tade kuu mushi*, "Yume no ukihashi"

Menéndez Cuspinera, M.

*Sasameyuki*

Meyer-Clason, Curt

*Tade kuu mushi*

Milenkovic, Dragan

"Shisei"

Miyamori Asatarô

"Shisei"

Miyamoto, Masao

"Shōnen," *Shunkinshō* (with Isiguro Teruhiko)

Montanaro, Paola

"Hyōfū," "Ken'etsukan"

Morris, Ivan

"Shisei"

Mottola, Cinzia

*Amachua kurabu*, *Hakuchūkigo*

Nieminen, Kai

*Sasameyuki*

Origlia, Lydia

"Akuma," "Futari no chigo," "Haha o kouru ki," "Itansha no kanashimi," *Manji*, "Norowareta gikyoku," *Otsuya koroshi*, "Zoku akuma"

Oseki, Konosuke

"Shisei"

Pál, Félix

"Yume no ukihashi"

# 8

# Selected Bibliography

Beillevaire, Patrick. *Le Japon en langue française—Ouvrages et articles publiés de 1850 à 1945*. Paris: Éditions Kimé, 1993.

Hérail, Francine. *Bibliographie japonaise (Éléments de bibliographie japonaise. Ouvrages traduits du japonais. Etudes en langues occidentales)*. Paris: POF, 1986.

International House of Japan Library, comp. *Modern Japanese Literature in Translation: A Bibliography*, 近代日本文学翻訳書目. Tokyo, New York and San Francisco: Kodansha International, 1979.

Japan P.E.N. Club, comp. *Japanese Literature in Foreign Languages 1945-1995*. N.p.: The Japan P.E.N. Club, 1997.

Stalph, Jürgen, Gisela Ogasa, and Dörte Puls. *Moderne japanische Literatur in deutscher Übersetzung: Eine Bibliographie der Jahre 1868-1994*, 日本近現代文学独訳目録. Bibliographische Arbeiten aus dem Deutschen Institut für Japanstudien der Philipp-Franz-von-Siebold-Stiftung, Band 3. München: Iudicium Verlag, 1995.

# A List of Films

# Based on Tanizaki's Works

compiled by

Maria Roberta Novielli

# Films Arranged in Chronological Order

LEGEND
Original story: oeuvre originale, soggetto, 原作
Director: réalisation, regia, 監督
Screenplay: scénario, sceneggiatura, 脚本
Cinematographer: images, fotografia, 撮影
Cast: interprètes, interpreti, 出演
Production company: production, casa di produzione, 制作会社
Silent: muet, muto, 無声
B/W: black and white, noir et blanc, bianco e nero, 白黒
C: color, en couleurs, colore, カラー
Duration : durée, durata, 時間
Retitled: When the film was retitled for foreign distribution with a title that diverges from the original, and when it is known, it is given here.

The first four titles are listed here because Tanizaki was deeply involved in the making of these films, not because they are based on one or other of his works. *Genji monogatari* by Yoshimura Kōzaburō (1951) has also been included, as Tanizaki was asked to supervise it.

1920
AMACHUA KURABU アマチュア倶楽部
Original story: Tanizaki Jun'ichirō 谷崎潤一郎
Director: Kurihara Kisaburō 栗原喜三郎 [Thomas Kurihara]
Screenplay: Tanizaki Jun'ichirō 谷崎潤一郎
Cinematographer: Inami Yoshimi 稲見興美
Cast: Ueno Hisao 上野久夫, Hayama Michiko 葉山三千子, Naitō Shiren 内藤紫漣, Kanda Chiyoko 神田千代子, Shiraishi Shikō 白石紫紅, Mita Saeko 三田小枝子, Takahashi Eiichi 高橋英一, Sugiura Ichirō 杉浦市郎, Takemura Nobuo 竹村信雄, Murakami Tetsuji 村上鉄次, Ōhashi Shōgo 大橋荘吾, Horikiri Shinnosuke 堀切森之助
Production company: Taikatsu 大活 (大正活映)
Silent
B/W
Five reels

1920
KATSUSHIKA SUNAKO 葛飾砂子
Original story: Izumi Kyōka 泉鏡花 , "Katsushika Sunako"

Director: Kurihara Kisaburō 栗原喜三郎
Screenplay: Tanizaki Jun'ichirō 谷崎潤一郎
Cinematographer: Inami Yoshimi 稲見興美
Cast: Toyoda Yurako 豊田由良子, Kamiyama Sango 上山珊瑚, Nora Kurao 野羅久良男 [pseud. Takahashi Eiichi 高橋英一]
Production company: Taikatsu 大活 (大正活映)
Silent
B/W
Three reels

1921
HINAMATSURI NO YORU 雛祭りの夜
Original story: Tanizaki Jun'ichirō 谷崎潤一郎
Director: Kurihara Kisaburō 栗原喜三郎
Screenplay: Tanizaki Jun'ichirō 谷崎潤一郎
Cinematographer: Inami Yoshimi 稲見興美
Cast: Hayama Michiko 葉山三千子, Tanizaki Ayuko 谷崎鮎子, Takahashi Eiichi 高橋英一
Production company: Taikatsu 大活 (大正活映)
Silent
B/W
Four reels

1921
JASEI NO IN 蛇性の婬
Original story: Ueda Akinari 上田秋成, *Jasei no in*
Director: Kurihara Kisaburō 栗原喜三郎
Screenplay: Tanizaki Jun'ichirō 谷崎潤一郎
Cinematographer: Inami Yoshimi 稲見興美
Cast: Benisawa Yōko 紅沢葉子, Okada Tokihiko 岡田時彦 [Takahashi Eiichi 高橋 英一]
Production company: Taikatsu 大活 (大正活映)
Silent
B/W
Ten reels

1922
OTSUYA KOROSHI お艶殺し
Original story: Tanizaki Jun'ichirō 谷崎潤一郎, *Otsuya koroshi*
Director: Nakagawa Shirō 中川紫郎
Screenplay: Nakagawa Shirō 中川紫郎
Cinematographer: Kawakami Yūki 川上勇気
Cast: Arashi Shōzō 嵐笑三, Jitsukawa Enshō 実川延松
Production company: Teikokukinema Kosaka 帝国キネマ小坂
Silent
B/W
[?]

1924
HONMOKU YAWA 本牧夜話
Original story: Tanizaki Jun'ichirō 谷崎潤一郎, "Honmoku yawa"

Director: Suzuki Kensaku 鈴木謙作
Screenplay: Tokita Eitarō 鴇田英太郎
Cinematographer: Tsukakoshi Shigeharu 塚越成治
Cast: Sakai Yoneko 酒井米子, Hayashi Masao 林正夫
Production company: Nikkatsu Kyōto 日活京都
Silent
B/W
Five reels

1925
OTSUYA KOROSHI お艶殺し
Original story: Tanizaki Jun'ichirō 谷崎潤一郎, *Otsuya koroshi*
Director: Sakata Shigenori 阪田重則
Screenplay: Sakata Shigenori 阪田重則
Cinematographer: Miki Minoru 三木尼稔, Iwaoka Senri 岩岡千里
Cast: Izumo Mikiko 出雲美樹子, Mori Eijirō 森英治郎, Sasaki Tsumoru 佐々木積, Miyajima Fumio 宮島啓夫, Hayashi Miki 林幹, Shirasaki Kikusaburō 白崎菊三郎
Production company: Tōa Kinema Kōyō 東亜キネマ甲陽
Silent
B/W
Seven reels

1934
OTSUYA KOROSHI お艶殺し
Original story: Tanizaki Jun'ichirō 谷崎潤一郎, *Otsuya koroshi*
Director: Tsuji Kichirō 辻吉朗
Screenplay: Fujimi Akira 富士見明
Cinematographer: Matsumura Teizō 松村禎三
Cast: Onoe Kikutarō 尾上菊太郎, Kuroda Kiyo 黒田記代
Production company: Nikkatsu Kyōto 日活京都
B/W
Eight reels

1935
OKOTO TO SASUKE お琴と佐助
Original story: Tanizaki Jun'ichirō 谷崎潤一郎, *Shunkinshō* 春琴抄
Director: Shimazu Yasujirō 島津保次郎
Screenplay: Shimazu Yasujirō 島津保次郎
Cinematographer: Kuwahara Takashi 桑原昂
Cast: Takada Kōkichi 高田浩吉, Tanaka Kinuyo 田中絹代, Saitō Tatsuo 斎藤達雄, Katsuragi Fumiko 葛城文子, Tsubouchi Yoshiko 坪内美子, Isono Akio 磯野秋雄, Kawamura Reikichi 河村黎吉, Tani Reikō 谷麗光, Matsui Junko 松井潤子, Mizushima Ryōtarō 水島亮太郎, Kamiyama Sōjin 上山草人
Production company: Shōchiku 松竹
B/W
94'

1942
OICHI NO KATA お市の方
Original story: Tanizaki Jun'ichirō 谷崎潤一郎, *Mōmoku monogatari* 盲目物語

Director: Nobuchi Akira 野淵昶
Screenplay: Nobuchi Akira 野淵昶
Cinematographer: Miki Shigeto 三木滋人
Cast: Araki Shinobu 荒木忍, Ōtomo Ryūtarō 大友柳太郎
Production company: Daiei 大映
B/W
88'

1949
CHIJIN NO AI 痴人の愛
Original story: Tanizaki Jun'ichirō 谷崎潤一郎, *Chijin no ai*
Director: Kimura Keigo 木村恵吾
Screenplay: Kimura Keigo 木村恵吾, Hatta Naoyuki 八田尚之
Cinematographer: Takemura Norikazu 竹村廉和
Cast: Kyō Machiko 京マチ子, Uno Jūkichi 宇野重吉, Mori Masayuki 森雅之, Kitakōchi Taeko 北河内妙子, Sugai Ichirō 菅井一郎, Shimizu Masao 清水将夫, Naraoka Tomoko 奈良岡朋子
Production company: Daiei Kyōto 大映京都
B/W
89'

1950
SASAMEYUKI 細雪
Original story: Tanizaki Jun'ichirō 谷崎潤一郎, *Sasameyuki*
Director: Abe Yutaka 阿部豊
Screenplay: Yasumi Toshio 八住利雄
Cinematographer: Yamanaka Susumu 山中進
Cast: Todoroki Yukiko 轟夕起子, Hanai Ranko 花井蘭子, Yamane Hisako 山根寿子, Takamine Hideko 高峰秀子
Production company: Shintōhō 新東宝
B/W
145'

1951
OTSUYA KOROSHI お艶殺し
Original story: Tanizaki Jun'ichirō 谷崎潤一郎, *Otsuya koroshi*
Director: Makino Masahiro マキノ雅弘
Screenplay: Yoda Yoshikata 依田義賢
Cinematographer: Miki Shigeto 三木滋人
Cast: Yamada Isuzu 山田五十鈴, Ichikawa Utaemon 市川右太衛門
Production company: Tōei 東映
B/W
96'

1951
GENJI MONOGATARI 源氏物語
Original story: Murasaki Shikibu 紫式部, *Genji monogatari*
Director: Yoshimura Kōzaburō 吉村公三郎
Screenplay: Shindō Kaneto 新藤兼人
Cinematographer: Sugiyama Kōhei 杉山公平

(supervision: Tanizaki Jun'ichirō 谷崎潤一郎)
Cast: Hasegawa Kazuo 長谷川一夫, Ōkōchi Denjirō 大河内伝次郎, Kogure Michiyo 木暮実千代, Mito Mitsuko 水戸光子, Kyō Machiko 京マチ子, Otowa Nobuko 乙羽信子, Hori Yūji 堀雄二
Production company: Daiei Kyōto 大映京都
B/W
130'

1951
OYŪSAMA お遊さま
Original story: Tanizaki Jun'ichirō 谷崎潤一郎, *Ashikari* 芦刈
Director: Mizoguchi Kenji 溝口健二
Screenplay: Yoda Yoshikata 依田義賢
Cinematographer: Miyagawa Kazuo 宮川一夫
Cast: Otowa Nobuko 乙羽信子, Tanaka Kinuyo 田中絹代, Hori Yūji 堀雄二, Yanagi Eijirō 柳永二郎, Shindō Eitarō 進藤英太郎
Production company: Daiei Kyōto 大映京都
B/W
95'
Retitled: Miss Oyu

1952
OKUNI TO GOHEI お国と五平
Original story: Tanizaki Jun'ichirō 谷崎潤一郎, *Okuni to Gohei*
Director: Naruse Mikio 成瀬巳喜男
Screenplay: Yasumi Toshio 八住利雄
Cinematographer: Yamada Kazuo 山田一夫
Cast: Ōtani Tomoemon 大谷友右衛門, Kogure Michiyo 木暮実千代
Production company: Tōhō 東宝
B/W
91'

1954
SHUNKIN MONOGATARI 春琴物語
Original story: Tanizaki Jun'ichirō 谷崎潤一郎, *Shunkinshō* 春琴抄
Director: Itō Daisuke 伊藤大輔
Screenplay: Yahiro Fuji 八尋不二
Cinematographer: Yamazaki Yasuichirō 山崎安一郎
Cast: Hanayagi Yoshiaki 花柳喜章, Kyō Machiko 京マチ子, Funakoshi Eiji 船越英二, Aoyama Sugisaku 青山杉作, Shindō Eitarō 進藤英太郎, Chiaki Minoru 千秋実
Production company: Daiei Tōkyō 大映東京
B/W
112'

1956
RANGIKU MONOGATARI 乱菊物語
Original story: Tanizaki Jun'ichirō 谷崎潤一郎, *Rangiku monogatari*
Director: Taniguchi Senkichi 谷口千吉
Screenplay: Yasumi Toshio 八住利雄
Cinematographer: Iimura Tadashi 飯村正

Cast: Yachigusa Kaoru 八千草薫, Ikebe Ryō 池部良
Production company: Tōhō 東宝
B/W
85'

1956
NEKO TO SHŌZŌ TO FUTARI NO ONNA 猫と庄造と二人のをんな
Original story: Tanizaki Jun'ichirō 谷崎潤一郎, *Neko to Shōzō to futari no onna*
Director: Toyoda Shirō 豊田四郎
Screenplay: Yasumi Toshio 八住利雄
Cinematographer: Miura Mitsuo 三浦光雄
Cast: Yamada Isuzu 山田五十鈴, Morishige Hisaya 森繁久弥, Naniwa Chieko 浪花千栄子, Kagawa Kyōko 香川京子, Minami Yūko 南悠子, Tanaka Haruo 田中春男
Production company: Tōkyō Eiga 東京映画
B/W
136'

1959
SASAMEYUKI 細雪
Original story: Tanizaki Jun'ichirō 谷崎潤一郎, *Sasameyuki*
Director: Shima Kōji 島耕二
Screenplay: Yasumi Toshio 八住利雄
Cinematographer: Ohara Jōji 小原譲治
Cast: Kyō Machiko 京マチ子, Todoroki Yukiko 轟夕起子, Yamamoto Fujiko 山本富士子, Kanō Junko 叶順子, Shin Kinzō 信欣三, Miyake Kuniko 三宅邦子, Sazanka Kyū 山茶花究, Negami Jun 根上淳
Production company: Daiei Tōkyō 大映東京
C
105'

1959
KAGI 鍵
Original story: Tanizaki Jun'ichirō 谷崎潤一郎, *Kagi*
Director: Ichikawa Kon 市川崑
Screenplay: Ichikawa Kon 市川崑, Wada Natto 和田夏十, Hasebe Keiji 長谷部慶次
Cinematographer: Miyagawa Kazuo 宮川一夫
Cast: Kyō Machiko 京マチ子, Nakamura Ganjirō 中村鴈治郎, Kanō Junko 叶順子, Nakadai Tatsuya 仲代達矢, Kitabayashi Tanie 北林谷栄, Sugai Ichirō 菅井一郎
Production company: Daiei Tōkyō 大映東京
C
107'
Retitled: Odd Obsession; L'étrange obsession

1960
CHIJIN NO AI 痴人の愛
Original story: Tanizaki Jun'ichirō 谷崎潤一郎, *Chijin no ai*
Director: Kimura Keigo 木村恵吾
Screenplay: Kimura Keigo 木村恵吾
Cinematographer: Ishida Hiroshi 石田博

Cast: Kanō Junko 叶順子, Funakoshi Eiji 船越英二, Tamiya Jirō 田宮二郎, Kawasaki Keizō 川崎敬三, Ishii Ryūichi 石井竜一, Ōkawa Osamu 大川修, Mikuni Ichirō 三国一朗, Tatara Jun 多々良純
Production company: Daiei Tōkyō 大映東京
C
89'

1961
OKOTO TO SASUKE お琴と佐助
Original story: Tanizaki Jun'ichirō 谷崎潤一郎, *Shunkinshō* 春琴抄
Director: Kinugasa Teinosuke 衣笠貞之助
Screenplay: Kinugasa Teinosuke 衣笠貞之助
Cinematographer: Murata Hiroshi 村田博
Cast: Hongō Kōjirō 本郷功次郎, Yamamoto Fujiko 山本富士子, Hanafu Tatsuo 花布辰男, Kahara Natsuko 賀原夏子, Kawasaki Keizō 川崎敬三, Chūjō Shizuo 中条静夫, Nakamura Nobuo 中村伸郎
Production company: Daiei Tōkyō 大映東京
C
94'
Retitled: The Koto-Player and Her Disciple

1962
FŪTEN RŌJIN NIKKI 瘋癲老人日記
Original story: Tanizaki Jun'ichirō 谷崎潤一郎, *Fūten rōjin nikki*
Director: Kimura Keigo 木村恵吾
Screenplay: Kimura Keigo 木村恵吾
Cinematographer: Munekawa Nobuo 宗川信夫
Cast: Wakao Ayako 若尾文子, Yamamura Sō 山村聡
Production company: Daiei Tōkyō 大映東京
B/W
99'

1963
DAIDOKORO TAIHEIKI 台所太平記
Original story: Tanizaki Jun'ichirō 谷崎潤一郎, *Daidokoro taiheiki*
Director: Toyoda Shirō 豊田四郎
Screenplay: Yasumi Toshio 八住利雄
Cinematographer: Okazaki Kōzō 岡崎宏三
Cast: Awashima Chikage 淡島千景, Morishige Hisaya 森繁久弥, Mori Mitsuko 森光子, Otowa Nobuko 乙羽信子, Kyōzuka Masako 京塚昌子, Awaji Keiko 淡路恵子, Mizutani Yoshie 水谷良重, Ikeuchi Junko 池内淳子, Ōzora Mayumi 大空真弓, Dan Reiko 団令子, Nakao Mie 中尾ミエ
Production company: Tōkyō Eiga - Tōhō 東京映画・東宝
C
110'
Retitled: The Maid Story

1964
HAKUJITSUMU 白日夢
Original story: Tanizaki Jun'ichirō 谷崎潤一郎, "Hakujitsumu"
Director: Takechi Tetsuji 武智鉄二
Screenplay: Takechi Tetsuji 武智鉄二

Cinematographer: Suganuma Masayoshi 菅沼政義
Cast: Ishihama Akira 石浜朗, Michi Kanako 路加奈子, Hanakawa Chōjūrō 花川蝶十郎, Matsui Yasuko 松井康子, Kobayashi Tokuji 小林十九二
Production company: Daisan Pro. – Shōchiku 第三プロ・松竹
C
94'
Retitled: Daydream

1964
MANJI 卍
Original story: Tanizaki Jun'ichirō 谷崎潤一郎, *Manji*
Director: Masumura Yasuzō 増村保造
Screenplay: Shindō Kaneto 新藤兼人
Cinematographer: Kobayashi Setsuo 小林節雄
Cast: Kishida Kyōko 岸田今日子, Wakao Ayako 若尾文子, Funakoshi Eiji 船越英二, Kawazu Yūsuke 川津裕介
Production company: Daiei Tōkyō 大映東京
C
91'
Retitled: Passion; All Mixed-up; Swastika; La svastica; La casa degli amori particolari

1964
KŌKEIMU 紅閨夢
Original story: Tanizaki Jun'ichirō 谷崎潤一郎, "Yanagiyu no jiken" 柳湯の事件
Director: Takechi Tetsuji 武智鉄二
Screenplay: Takechi Tetsuji 武智鉄二
Cinematographer: Inaba Tadashi 稲葉直
Cast: Kawaguchi Hideko 川口秀子, Shigeyama Sennojō 茂山千之丞
Production company: Daisan Pro. – Shōchiku 第三プロ・松竹
C
76'

1965
AKUTŌ 悪党
Original story: Tanizaki Jun'ichirō 谷崎潤一郎, *Kaoyo* 顔世
Director: Shindō Kaneto 新藤兼人
Screenplay: Shindō Kaneto 新藤兼人
Cinematographer: Kuroda Kiyomi 黒田清巳
Cast: Kishida Kyōko 岸田今日子, Ozawa Eitarō 小沢栄太郎, Otowa Nobuko 乙羽信子, Kimura Isao 木村功, Tonoyama Taiji 殿山泰司, Ōki Shōji 大木正司, Uno Jūkichi 宇野重吉
Production company: Tōhō - Tōkyō Eiga - Kindai Eiga Kyōkai 東宝・東京映画・近代映画協会
B/W
119'
Retitled: Conquest

1966
IREZUMI 刺青
Original story: Tanizaki Jun'ichirō 谷崎潤一郎, "Shisei" 刺青
Director: Masumura Yasuzō 増村保造

Screenplay: Shindō Kaneto 新藤兼人
Cinematographer: Miyagawa Kazuo 宮川一夫
Cast: Hasegawa Akio 長谷川明男, Wakao Ayako 若尾文子, Yamamoto Gaku 山本学, Satō Kei 佐藤慶, Suga Fujio 須賀不二男, Uchida Asao 内田朝雄, Fujiwara Reiko 藤原礼子
Production company: Daiei Kyōto 大映京都
C
86'
Retitled: The Spider Tattoo; Il tatuaggio; Le Tatouage

1967
DARAKU SURU ONNA 堕落する女
Original story: Tanizaki Jun'ichirō 谷崎潤一郎, *Aisureba koso* 愛すればこそ
Director: Yoshimura Kōzaburō 吉村公三郎
Screenplay: Shindō Kaneto 新藤兼人
Cinematographer: Satō Masamichi 佐藤昌道
Cast: Hosokawa Toshiyuki 細川俊之, Kuwano Miyuki 桑野みゆき, Tamura Takahiro 田村高広
Production company: Kindai Eikyō - Shōchiku 近代映協・松竹
B/W
101'

1967
CHIJIN NO AI 痴人の愛
Original story: Tanizaki Jun'ichirō 谷崎潤一郎, *Chijin no ai*
Director: Masumura Yasuzō 増村保造
Screenplay: Ikeda Ichirō 池田一朗
Cinematographer: Kobayashi Setsuo 小林節雄
Cast: Ozawa Shōichi 小沢昭一, Yasuda Michiyo 安田道代, Tamura Masakazu 田村正和, Kuraishi Isao 倉石功, Murase Sachiko 村瀬幸子, Uchida Asao 内田朝雄, Konno Yuka 紺野ユカ, Kiyokawa Tamae 清川玉枝
Production company: Daiei Tōkyō 大映東京
C
92'
Retitled: La chatte japonaise; La gatta giapponese

1969
ONI NO SUMU YAKATA 鬼の棲む館
Original story: Tanizaki Jun'ichirō 谷崎潤一郎, *Mumyō to Aizen* 無明と愛染
Director: Misumi Kenji 三隅研次
Screenplay: Shindō Kaneto 新藤兼人
Cinematographer: Miyagawa Kazuo 宮川一夫
Cast: Aratama Michiyo 新珠三千代, Katsu Shintarō 勝新太郎, Takamine Hideko 高峰秀子, Satō Kei 佐藤慶, Gomi Ryūtarō 五味龍太郎
Production company: Daiei Kyōto 大映京都
C
76'
Retitled: Devil's Temple

1970
ONNA GOKUAKU CHŌ おんあ極悪帖
Original story: Tanizaki Jun'ichirō 谷崎潤一郎, *Kyōfu jidai* 恐怖時代
Director: Ikehiro Kazuo 池広一夫
Screenplay: Hoshikawa Seiji 星川清司
Cinematographer: Kajitani Toshio 梶谷俊男
Cast: Tamura Masakazu 田村正和, Yasuda Michiyo 安田道代
Production company: Daiei Kyōto 大映京都
C
84'

1972
SANKA 讃歌
Original story: Tanizaki Jun'ichirō 谷崎潤一郎, *Shunkinshō* 春琴抄
Director: Shindō Kaneto 新藤兼人
Screenplay: Shindō Kaneto 新藤兼人
Cinematographer: Kuroda Kiyomi 黒田清己
Cast: Watanabe Tokuko 渡辺督子, Kawarasaki Jirō 河原崎次郎, Otowa Nobuko 乙羽信子, Takechi Tetsuji 武智鉄二, Hatsui Kotoe 初井言榮, Tonoyama Taiji 殿山泰司, Harada Daijirō 原田大二郎, Toura Mutsuhiro 戸浦六宏, Kusano Daigo 草野大悟, Motoyama Kakuko 本山可久子, Shindō Kaneto 新藤兼人
Production company: Kindai Eiga Kyōkai - ATG 近代映画協会・ATG
C
112'

1974
KAGI 鍵
Original story: Tanizaki Jun'ichirō 谷崎潤一郎, *Kagi*
Director: Kumashiro Tatsumi 神代辰巳
Screenplay: Kumashiro Tatsumi 神代辰巳
Cinematographer: Himeda Masahisa 姫田真佐久
Cast: Aresa Yuki 荒砂ゆき, Kanze Hideo 観世栄夫, Watanabe Tokuko 渡辺督子, Kawarasaki Kenzō 河原崎健三, Katō Yoshi 加藤嘉
Production company: Nikkatsu 日活
C
90'

1976
SHUNKINSHŌ 春琴抄
Original story: Tanizaki Jun'ichirō 谷崎潤一郎, *Shunkinshō*
Director: Nishikawa Katsumi 西河克巳
Screenplay: Nishikawa Katsumi 西河克巳, Kinugasa Teinosuke 衣笠貞之助
Cinematographer: Satō Kenji 佐藤憲治
Cast: Miura Tomokazu 三浦友和, Yamaguchi Momoe 山口百恵, Tsugawa Masahiko 津川雅彦, Nakamura Takeya 中村竹弥, Kazami Akiko 風見章子, Nakamura Nobuo 中村伸郎
Production company: Hori Kikaku Seisaku ホリ企画制作
C
97'

1980
NAOMI ナオミ
Original story: Tanizaki Jun'ichirō, *Chijin no ai* 痴人の愛
Director: Takabayashi Yōichi 高林陽一
Screenplay: Takabayashi Yōichi 高林陽一
Cinematographer: Takamura Kuratarō 高村倉太郎
Cast: Saitō Makoto 斎藤真, Mizuhara Yūki 水原ゆう紀
Production company: Tōkyō Central Film 東京セントラルフィルム
C
104'

1981
HAKUJITSUMU 白日夢
Original story: Tanizaki Jun'ichirō 谷崎潤一郎, "Hakujitsumu"
Director: Takechi Tetsuji 武智鉄二
Screenplay: Takechi Tetsuji 武智鉄二
Cinematographer: Takada Akira 高田昭
Cast: Aizome Kyōko 愛染恭子, Satō Kei 佐藤慶, Kawaguchi Sae 川口小枝, Sugumi Takeyoshi 勝然武美, Tonoyama Taiji 殿山泰司
Production company: Fuji Eiga - Takechi Production 富士映画・武智プロダクション
C
110'
Retitled: Daydream

1983
OIRAN 華魁
Original story: Tanizaki Jun'ichirō 谷崎潤一郎, "Jinmenso" 人面疽
Director: Takechi Tetsuji 武智鉄二
Screenplay: Takechi Tetsuji 武智鉄二
Cinematographer: Takada Akira 高田昭
Cast: Itō Takashi 伊藤高, Shinnōzuka Takako 新王塚貴子, Mashiba Satoshi 真柴さとし, Kawaguchi Sae 川口小枝, Yūzaki Midori 夕崎碧
Production company: Takechi Ogawa Production 武智・小川プロダクション
C
113'

1983
MANJI 卍
Original story: Tanizaki Jun'ichirō 谷崎潤一郎, *Manji*
Director: Yokoyama Hiroto 横山博人
Screenplay: Baba Masaru 馬場当
Cinematographer: Nakajima Tōru 中島徹
Cast: Takase Haruna 高瀬春奈, Higuchi Kanako 樋口可南子, Harada Yoshio 原田芳雄
Production company: Yokoyama Hiroto Production 横山博人プロダクション
C
98'

1983
KAGI 鍵
Original story: Tanizaki Jun'ichirō 谷崎潤一郎, *Kagi*
Director: Kimata Akitaka 木俣尭喬
Screenplay: Kimata Akitaka 木俣尭喬
Cinematographer: Kimata Akitaka 木俣尭喬
Cast: Matsuo Kayo 松尾嘉代, Okada Masumi 岡田真澄, Egami Shingo 江上慎吾, Taguchi Yoshio 田口由緒
Production company: Otik International - Wakamatsu Pro. オティクインターナショナル・若松プロ
C
107'

1983
SASAMEYUKI 細雪
Original story: Tanizaki Jun'ichirō 谷崎潤一郎, *Sasameyuki*
Director: Ichikawa Kon 市川崑
Screenplay: Ichikawa Kon 市川崑
Cinematographer: Hasegawa Kiyoshi 長谷川清
Cast: Yoshinaga Sayuri 吉永小百合, Sakuma Yoshiko 佐久間良子, Kotegawa Yūko 古手川祐子, Kishi Keiko 岸恵子, Ishizaka Kōji 石坂浩二, Itami Jūzō 伊丹十三, Tsuji Kazunaga 辻万長
Production company: Tōhō Eiga 東宝映画
C
140'
Retitled: The Makioka Sisters

1983
LA CHIAVE
Original story: Tanizaki Jun'ichirō 谷崎潤一郎, *Kagi* 鍵
Director: Tinto Brass
Screenplay: Paolo Biagetti
Cinematographer: Silvano Ippoliti
Cast: Stefania Sandrelli, Frank Finlay, Franco Branciaroli, Maria Grazia Bon, Barbara Cupisti, Armando Marra, Marina Cecchetelli, Maria Pia Colonnello
Production company: San Francisco Film
C
100'

1984
IREZUMI 刺青
Original story: Tanizaki Jun'ichirō 谷崎潤一郎, "Shisei" 刺青
Director: Sone Chūsei 曽根中生
Screenplay: Nasu Machiko 那須真知子
Cinematographer: Mori Masaru 森勝
Cast: Sawada Kazumi 沢田和美, Itō Sakiko 伊藤咲子
Production company: Nikkatsu 日活
C
77'

1985
INTERNO BERLINESE
Original story: Tanizaki Jun'ichirō 谷崎潤一郎, *Manji* 卍
Director: Liliana Cavani
Screenplay: Luciano Ricceri
Cinematographer: Dante Spinotti
Cast: Gudrun Landgrebe, Kevin McNally, Takaki Mio, Massimo Girotti, Philippe Leroy, William Berger
Production company: Menahem Golan e Yoram Globus, Cannon Pr.; Italian Int. Film; Italia-R.F.T.
C
120'

1987
HAKUJITSUMU 2 白日夢 2
Original story: Tanizaki Jun'ichirō 谷崎潤一郎, "Hakujitsumu"
Director: Takechi Tetsuji 武智鉄二
Screenplay: Takechi Tetsuji 武智鉄二
Cinematographer: Sugimura Hiroaki 杉村博章
Cast: Aizome Kyōko 愛染恭子, Kirinami Chizu 霧波千種寿, Hayami Kenji 速水健二, Suga Kantarō 菅館太郎
Production company: Daisan Pro. 第三プロ
C
90'
Retitled: Daydream 2, Captured for Sex

1997
KAGI 鍵
Original story: Tanizaki Jun'ichirō 谷崎潤一郎, *Kagi*
Director: Ikeda Toshiharu 池田敏春
Screenplay: Shiratori Akane 白鳥あかね, Kagawa Masahito 香川まさひと, Ikeda Toshiharu 池田敏春
Cinematographer: Maeda Yonezō 前田米造
Cast: Kawashima Naomi 川島なお美, Emoto Akira 柄本明, Ōsawa Mikio 大沢樹生, Tsuji Kaori 辻香緒里, Imai Kenji 今井健二, Mitani Noboru 三谷昇, Niki Terumi 二木てるみ, Hirooka Yuriko 広岡由里子
Production company: Tōei 東映
C
95'

1997
MANJI 卍
Original story: Tanizaki Jun'ichirō 谷崎潤一郎, *Manji*
Director: Hattori Mitsunori 服部光則
Screenplay: Miyamoto Jun みやもとじゅん
Cinematographer: Nishikubo Korehiro 西久保維宏
Cast: Sakagami Kaori 坂上香織, Mayumi Michiko 真弓倫子, Hiraizumi Shigeru 平泉成, Shima Daisuke 嶋大輔, Hara Chisako 原知佐子
Production company: Gaga Productions
C
80'

# Films Arranged by Film Title

*Akutō* (Shindō Kaneto, 1965)
*Chijin no ai* (Kimura Keigo, 1949)
*Chijin no ai* (Kimura Keigo, 1960)
*Chijin no ai* (Masumura Yasuzō, 1967)
*Daidokoro taiheiki* (Toyoda Shirō, 1963)
*Daraku suru onna* (Yoshimura Kōzaburō, 1967)
*Fūten rōjin nikki* (Kimura Keigo, 1962)
*Hakujitsumu* (Takechi Tetsuji, 1964)
*Hakujitsumu* (Takechi Tetsuji, 1981)
*Hakujitsumu 2* (Takechi Tetsuji, 1987)
*Honmoku yawa* (Suzuki Kensaku, 1924)
*Interno berlinese* (Liliana Cavani, 1985)
*Irezumi* (Masumura Yasuzō, 1966)
*Irezumi* (Sone Chūsei, 1984)
*Kagi* (Ichikawa Kon, 1959)
*Kagi* (Kumashiro Tatsumi, 1974)
*Kagi* (Kimata Akitaka, 1983)
*Kagi* (Ikeda Toshiharu, 1997)
*Kōkeimu* (Takechi Tetsuji, 1964)
*La chiave* (Tinto Brass, 1983)
*Manji* (Masumura Yasuzō, 1964)
*Manji* (Yokoyama Hiroto, 1983)
*Manji* (Hattori Mitsunori, 1997)
*Naomi* (Takabayashi Yōichi, 1980)
*Neko to Shōzō to futari no onna* (Toyoda Shirō, 1956)
*Oichi no kata* (Nobuchi Akira, 1942)
*Oiran* (Takechi Tetsuji, 1983)
*Okoto to Sasuke* (Shimazu Yasujirō, 1935)
*Okoto to Sasuke* (Kinugasa Teinosuke, 1961)
*Okuni to Gohei* (Naruse Mikio, 1952)
*Oni no sumu yakata* (Misumi Kenji, 1969)
*Onna gokuaku chō* (Ikehiro Kazuo, 1970)
*Otsuya koroshi* (Nakagawa Shirō, 1922)
*Otsuya koroshi* (Sakata Shigenori, 1925)
*Otsuya koroshi* (Tsuji Kichirō, 1934)

*Otsuya koroshi* (Makino Masahiro, 1951)
*Oyūsama* (Mizoguchi Kenji, 1951)
*Rangiku monogatari* (Taniguchi Senkichi, 1956)
*Sanka* (Shindō Kaneto, 1972)
*Sasameyuki* (Abe Yutaka, 1950)
*Sasameyuki* (Shima Kōji, 1959)
*Sasameyuki* (Ichikawa Kon, 1983)
*Shunkin monogatari* (Itō Daisuke, 1954)
*Shunkinshō* (Nishikawa Katsumi, 1976)

# Films Arranged by Title of Original Work

*Aisureba koso*
*Daraku suru onna* (Yoshimura Kōzaburō, 1967)

*Ashikari*
*Oyūsama* (Mizoguchi Kenji, 1951)

*Chijin no ai*
*Chijin no ai* (Kimura Keigo, 1949)
*Chijin no ai* (Kimura Keigo, 1960)
*Chijin no ai* (Masumura Yasuzō, 1967)
*Naomi* (Takabayashi Yōichi, 1980)

*Daidokoro taiheiki*
*Daidokoro taiheiki* (Toyoda Shirō, 1963)

*Fūten rōjin nikki*
*Fūten rōjin nikki* (Kimura Keigo, 1962)

"Hakujitsumu"
*Hakujitsumu* (Takechi Tetsuji, 1964)
*Hakujitsumu* (Takechi Tetsuji, 1981)
*Hakujitsumu 2* (Takechi Tetsuji, 1987)

"Honmoku yawa"
*Honmoku yawa* (Suzuki Kensaku, 1924)

"Jinmensō"
*Oiran* (Takechi Tetsuji, 1983)

*Kagi*
*Kagi* (Ichikawa Kon, 1959)
*Kagi* (Kumashiro Tatsumi, 1974)
*Kagi* (Kimata Akitaka, 1983)
*La chiave* (Tinto Brass, 1983)
*Kagi* (Ikeda Toshiharu, 1997)

*Kaoyo*
*Akutō* (Shindō Kaneto, 1965)

*Kyōfu jidai*
*Onna gokuaku chō* (Ikehiro Kazuo, 1970)

*Manji*
*Manji* (Masumura Yasuzō, 1964)
*Manji* (Yokoyama Hiroto, 1983)
*Interno berlinese* (Liliana Cavani, 1985)
*Manji* (Hattori Mitsunori, 1997)

*Mōmoku monogatari*
*Oichi no kata* (Nobuchi Akira, 1942)

*Mumyō to Aizen*
*Oni no sumu yakata* (Misumi Kenji, 1969)

*Neko to Shōzō to futari no onna*
*Neko to Shōzō to futari no onna* (Toyoda Shirō, 1956)

*Okuni to Gohei*
*Okuni to Gohei* (Naruse Mikio, 1952)

*Otsuya koroshi*
*Otsuya koroshi* (Nakagawa Shirō, 1922)
*Otsuya koroshi* (Sakata Shigenori, 1925)
*Otsuya koroshi* (Tsuji Kichirō, 1934)
*Otsuya koroshi* (Makino Masahiro, 1951)

*Rangiku monogatari*
*Rangiku monogatari* (Taniguchi Senkichi, 1956)

*Sasameyuki*
*Sasameyuki* (Abe Yutaka, 1950)
*Sasameyuki* (Shima Kōji, 1959)
*Sasameyuki* (Ichikawa Kon, 1983)

"Shisei"
*Irezumi* (Masumura Yasuzō, 1966)
*Irezumi* (Sone Chūsei, 1984)

*Shunkinshō*
*Okoto to Sasuke* (Shimazu Yasujirō, 1935)
*Shunkin monogatari* (Itō Daisuke, 1954)
*Okoto to Sasuke* (Kinugasa Teinosuke, 1961)
*Sanka* (Shindō Kaneto, 1972)
*Shunkinshō* (Nishikawa Katsumi, 1976)

"Yanagiyu no jiken"
*Kōkeimu* (Takechi Tetsuji, 1964)